Teachers Behaving Badly?

Teachers Behaving Badly?

Dilemmas for school leaders

Kate Myers
with Graham Clayton,
David James and Jim O'Brien

RoutledgeFalmer
Taylor & Francis Group

LONDON AND NEW YORK

First published 2005 by RoutledgeFalmer
2 Park Square, Milton Park, Abingdon, Oxon OX14 4RN

Simultaneously published in the USA and Canada
by RoutledgeFalmer
270 Madison Ave, New York, NY 10016

RoutledgeFalmer is an imprint of the Taylor & Francis Group

© 2005 Kate Myers for chapters, editorial material and selection,
individual chapters the contributors

Typeset in Sabon by Keystroke, Jacaranda Lodge, Wolverhampton
Printed and bound in Great Britain by TJ International Ltd, Padstow,
Cornwall

British Library Cataloguing in Publication Data
A catalogue record for this book is available from the British Library

Library of Congress Cataloging in Publication Data
Myers, Kate.
    Teachers behaving badly? : dilemmas for school leaders / Kate Myers.
        p. cm.
    Includes bibliographical references and index.
    ISBN 0–415–32115–8 (pbk. : alk. paper)
        1. Teachers–Professional ethics–Great Britain. 2. Teacher-student
relationships–Great Britain. 3. Educational leadership–Great Britain. I. Title.
    LB1779.M94 2005
    194′.937–dc22

                                                    20904011026

ISBN 0–415–32115–8

This book is dedicated to my family, especially Dorothy, Peter, Marsha, Mark, Paul, Georgina and Sarah Myers and for the new generation of teachers and classroom assistants, especially Peter and Chloe Field

Contents

About the authors

Kate Myers is Emeritus Professor of the University of Keele. She is a senior associate of the Leadership *for* Learning Network at the University of Cambridge and an adviser for the London Challenge. She has been a teacher, an advisory teacher, an inspector, an Associate Director of the International School Effectiveness and Improvement Centre, Institute of Education and has directed equal opportunities and school improvement projects. Her books include *Genderwatch! After the ERA*, 1992; *School Improvement in Practice: The Schools Make a Difference Project*, 1996; *No Quick Fixes: Perspectives on Schools in Difficulty*, 1998, co-editor with Louise Stoll; *Effective School Leaders: How to Evaluate and Improve Your Leadership Potential*, written with John MacBeath, 1999; *Whatever Happened to Equal Opportunities in Schools? Gender Equality Initiatives in Education*, an edited collection published in 2000; *The Intelligent School* with Barbara MacGilchrist and Jane Reed, 2004; and co-editor, with John MacBeath, of the RoutledgeFalmer series 'What's In It for Schools . . . '.

Graham Clayton is Senior Solicitor at the National Union of Teachers, England and Wales. Graham joined the NUT as its second solicitor in 1976 and took over as Senior Solicitor in 1987. He is responsible for all the legal aspects of the union's work. Graham has appeared as an advocate in several reported decisions of the Employment Appeals Tribunal and as solicitor instructing counsel in several High Court, Court of Appeal, House of Lords and European Court of Justice cases. He leads a team of 14 lawyers in a uniquely structured service delivered to NUT members and is directly involved in the development of education laws commenting from the union's point of view on proposed new laws and drafting and submitting amendments to proposed new legislation for consideration by the House of Commons and House of Lords Committees. He is a contributor to Butterworths' *Education Law Manual*, the author of numerous articles for the union's in-house magazine, *The Teacher* and other legal and education journals, and has made several TV and radio appearances as a commentator on education law issues. He is a graduate of Jesus College, Cambridge.

David James has been the Professional Standards Manager with the General Teaching Council since its inauguration in 2000. He started his professional life as a teacher of English before moving into LEAs. He was the Head of Education Personnel Services in a Midlands LEA for 12 years and has run personnel management courses for headteachers on a freelance basis. He writes here in a personal capacity.

Jim O'Brien is Vice Dean of the Moray House School of Education in the University of Edinburgh. He has been a teacher, lecturer in guidance and pastoral care, and Director of In-Service with responsibility for teacher CPD. He has contributed to several national development projects in Scotland including appraisal and review, the Scottish Qualification for Headship (SQH) and recently the development of the Standard for Chartered Teacher and associated pilot programmes. He has published in the fields of CPD, leadership and management and school improvement. A current focus is on multimedia CPD resources for teachers and he has co-authored a number of CD-roms and online materials including *Dealing with Disruption* 2001; *Issues in School Improvement*, 2002; *Co-ordinating Staff Development*, 1999; *Raising the Standard: Study Support*, 1999. His co-authored books include *Performance Management in Education: Improving Practice*, 2002 and *School Leadership*, 2003.

Acknowledgements

Part of this book originally appeared in the *International Journal of Leadership in Education: Theory and Practice*, vol. 5, no. 4 (2002) in an article called 'Dilemmas of Leadership: sexuality and schools'.

Thanks are due to David Frost, Andy Hargreaves, Ian Jamieson, John MacBeath and Pat Mahoney for their comments on drafts of the article. For the book, thanks to Gillies MacKinnon for permission to use the cartoon 'He's very nice, but he's a teacher'. Much appreciation goes to the anonymous contributors who shared their stories with me and to Sue Adler, Meryl Thompson, Frances Widdowson, Sue Goldie and Mike Raleigh for help with various facets of the book. Particular thanks and appreciation to Alan Richardson and Sarah Myers.

Introduction

When Keith worked with Jenny – and Lisa

Dramatis personae

Keith: Head of house – married to Jenny.
Jenny: Part-time teacher – married to Keith.
Lisa: Head of faculty – (mid-30s) married to non-teacher.
All three work at the same school.

My suspicions were first raised about the possibility of an affair when Keith and Lisa started behaving in a slightly flirtatious manner and always sitting together at curriculum and pastoral meetings. One of my deputies then reported that Keith had been spending a lot of time in another subject department office at lunchtime and after school. As he did not teach that subject, this new behaviour pattern was again an indicator to me (and probably the rest of the staff) that something was going on. Normally this would be of no concern, or interest, but in this case Keith was not only married but his wife Jenny was also a member of our staff. Lisa was also married but not to a teacher or anyone connected with the school.

Around the same time Jenny confided in her colleague and close friend Jane that she had suspected her husband Keith had been having an affair. When confronted, he had admitted to it being someone at school.

Jane came to see me and explained the situation as she understood it. It had been my intention to speak to Jenny initially, prior to speaking to Keith and Lisa. Later that day Lisa came to see me to 'clarify rumours you may have heard'. She assured me that a friendship had grown out of the school skiing trip, that Keith's marriage was in difficulties and that she had been providing a listening ear at his request. The relationship had gone as far as two meetings in a park after work – it was not physical.

I discussed this with my two female deputies and they agreed to meet with Jenny to hear her account of events. Their report from this meeting was that there had been marriage difficulties, but that Keith had been open with Jenny and that a sexual relationship had developed. Furthermore, when asked about the future, Keith had indicated to Jenny that if Lisa wanted him, he would be prepared to leave Jenny and their family, to pursue a long term relationship with Lisa – in short, the decision was in Lisa's hands.

Following this meeting Jenny came to see me, understandably very upset, with a number of concerns. Primarily that Lisa was not being truthful, that Keith and Jenny had a child joining the school in September – and that Keith had moved out of the family home. We discussed the practical things the school could do to protect the interests of all parties – I made guarantees about Lisa not being the teacher or form tutor of the prospective student – about Lisa not being a member of Keith's house team – of Lisa and Jenny not being in the same house team and of Jenny not being used for cover for Lisa's lessons. At this stage I was keen to point out that Lisa had not acknowledged the full extent of the allegations.

My two deputies met with Lisa to seek further clarification – she explained that the full extent of the allegations was true – they suggested Lisa see me immediately. I met with Lisa the following day – she apologised for lying – explaining that at that time she was unsure of what Keith had told his wife. Lisa assured me that the affair was over and that she had no interest in pursuing any relationship with Keith. I talked through an appropriate protocol and way forward in terms of Lisa's day-to-day professional conduct – this she accepted.

I met again with Jenny to inform her that Lisa now acknowledged the full extent of the relationship and accepted the agreed way forward in terms of conduct in school. By this time Jenny had taken it upon herself to visit Lisa's home and to confront her husband about the affair. In addition she had confronted Lisa at the end of school in public view – this led to the raising of voices but was fortunately not witnessed by any students. I explained that it was in everyone's interest that this matter was dealt with as professionally as possible and that any observations, allegations or complaints from students, parents or governors could have very serious consequences.

I spoke to Lisa again who confirmed the home visit and explained that she had a very understanding husband and that they were working to repair their damaged relationship.

Later that day I spoke to Keith who completely acknowledged the affair and agreed with the proposed way forward in terms of professional conduct. He was unsure at this stage whether or not he would be able to repair the relationship with Jenny or whether he would be able to move back in to the family home.

Just under 12 months on . . .

The school has honoured its commitments to all parties – Keith and Jenny are back together as a family unit – Lisa reports that she and her husband are 'getting back to normal'. There have been no complaints or questions from students, parents or governors. There was no ski trip!

(Anonymous submission from a secondary headteacher)

About this book

Preparation for school leadership has improved immensely over the last few years. Even so, many new leaders would feel inadequate and unprepared to deal with the real-life situation described above. Sex and sexuality are not often mentioned on leadership courses or in the manuals yet although not all leaders will have to confront the above scenario they are likely to be faced with similar complex dilemmas of a sexual nature that demand a quick response. Sometimes the situations would be humorous if they were in other contexts and sometimes as the one above (and others described in the book, one of which ended in manslaughter), they are potentially explosive. The responses of those dealing with these situations will need to take into account changes in social attitudes as well as the situation of the individuals concerned. If lucky, they may be able to draw on previous professional experiences to help clarify reactions, but contexts are often particular and different enough to require new thinking.

This book has been written for school leaders, and those working with schools, who have to deal with issues connected with teachers and sexuality. It is not in the main about paedophiles nor is it about inappropriate sexual behaviour, such as sexual bullying, manifested between pupils. Much has already been written on both these areas and there is plenty of advice available for school leaders who have to deal with incidents arising from these issues.

Here we are concerned about sexual behaviour that may occur between adults working in and connected to the school, and teacher/older pupil relations, initiated by both parties. Leaders faced with trying to sort out these issues find that they are not always clear-cut; often there are no easy resolutions; and the consequences may be potentially explosive – for the individuals concerned, for the school and for the community.

Sexuality in schools can involve adults and/or pupils. *Teachers Behaving Badly?* addresses sexual relations that may occur between adults (consensual and not) as well as those that may occur between teachers and pupils (teachers to pupils and pupils to teachers). Most of the cases discussed involve teachers, though of course, these issues can affect support staff employed by the school and other adults involved with schooling, such as governors, local authority employees and even Ofsted inspectors. Real life scenarios are included throughout.

The book is divided into two parts. Part I discusses some of the issues and Part II suggests some solutions.

Part I: some issues

The first half of the book deals with the issues that can and do arise in schools.

Chapter 1, 'Changing times', considers how times change and how values change with those times. What was considered inappropriate behaviour at the beginning of the twentieth century is no longer a view shared by the whole population. For example, attitudes to marriage, sex before marriage, divorce and illegitimacy have changed considerably in the recent past. A leader dealing with the situation cited at the beginning of this chapter some fifty years ago would almost certainly have insisted on all, or some, of those involved, leaving the school. There would be issues about the sanctity of marriage and the expected behaviour of teachers as role models for their young charges. An important question for school leaders is: should their values change with the times or should they be based on a personal value and belief system? Another question many have to address is what to do if they are leading a school in a community that does not share their own values, e.g. a homophobic community that will not tolerate 'out' gay or lesbian teachers.

Chapter 2, 'Amongst equals', is about the sexual behaviour of teachers. The question is posed for school leaders about when, if at all, sexual relations amongst their staff are their business. At what point should staff who are involved in a relationship with a colleague, declare potential conflicts of interest? Should teachers be accountable for their behaviour outside of school hours? How do school leaders manage the difficult boundary between what is properly the private concern of their staff and what is, whether properly or not, in the public domain?

In chapter 3 'The age of innocence', sexual behaviour between pupils and teacher is discussed. It is not uncommon for adults to act in a sexual manner as part of their 'social script' and teachers are no different here from the rest of the population. Both flirting and sexual bullying exists in many schools and are sometimes strategies utilised for disciplinary purposes. Pupils are not averse to trying out these strategies with their teachers too. They are often learning their 'sexual script' and will try out these sexual behaviours particularly with young and vulnerable staff. How do school leaders decide what behaviour is acceptable and what is 'off-limits'? For example, how do they deal with a consensual, genuine relationship between an 18-year-old student and a 22-year-old teacher (now a criminal offence)?

Part II: some solutions

The second half of the book addresses ways of dealing with some of the situations discussed in the first half. These issues are examined in connection with the law and the General Teachers Council. In the final chapter some advice is offered as to how professional development courses and programmes can consider these issues.

In chapter 4, 'Brief encounters: dealing with the law', Graham Clayton explores why there is law to deal with sexual relationships involving children and young people, directly and indirectly. He discusses the beliefs in our society which give rise to law and what objectives the law serves. He explores what the law requires of teachers both in terms of the protection they must give to children and in the example they are required to set.

In the following chapter 'Cracking the code', chapter 5, David James discusses some of the challenges which arise for school leaders and managers in handling the conduct and behaviour of staff in schools. He explores the procedures that apply at individual school level, on the part of the employer and at national level. The aim is to give school leaders a sense of what may be required of them in managing staff conduct issues and how their actions fit into the wider perspective of how the profession is regulated nationally. In the course of describing these practicalities, he recognises that ethical dilemmas may lie at the heart of many of the issues school leaders face.

Chapter 6, 'Be prepared', suggests that rather than waiting for critical incidents to occur, school leaders could anticipate situations and plan for how they would like to react, rather than be surprised by a complex situation that demands a quick response. The experience of those who have had to deal with difficult situations is recounted.

In the final chapter, 'Sexing up the flip charts', Jim O'Brien offers ways that schools, LEAs and facilitators of courses for current and aspiring school leaders could provide professional development that gives teachers and school leaders the opportunity to explore some of the issues discussed in this book.

We hope this book will help current and aspiring school leaders think through situations they may encounter, and be prepared to face them with confidence, integrity and humanity.

Kate Myers
March 2004

Part I

Some issues

Chapter 1

Changing times

Kate Myers

> Freud alerted social scientists to the presence of sexuality from the earliest age and stressed its importance in people's lives. But, . . . the tendency in schools is to pretend it does not really exist even though it is visible in so many different facets.
>
> (Wolpe, 1988, p. 158)

> There is strong evidence to support the claim that sexual values, attitudes and behaviours have changed more and become more diverse in the United Kingdom and other western countries in the last half-century than they did in the previous five hundred.
>
> (Halstead and Reiss, 2003, p. 17)

> Schools are sites where sexual and other identities are developed, practised and actively produced.
>
> (Epstein and Johnson, 1998, p. 2)

At the beginning of the twenty-first century it is not always straightforward when, if at all, the sexual behaviour of teachers is or should become a concern of the head. There are confusing messages about the extent to which teachers (and headteachers) are expected to be moral exemplars and role models. Heterosexuals, homosexuals, bisexuals, transsexuals and transvestites – any of whom could be practising or celibate – will be found amongst teachers (and headteachers), as in the rest of the population. Most of the time the sexuality and sexual behaviour of teachers and headteachers will have nothing to do with the institution in which they work, but on occasions this distinction may not prevail. *Teachers Behaving Badly?* considers issues such as:

- Personal or professional?
- Individual beliefs vs. community beliefs.

For example, at what point do (or should) private matters become public ones? At what point do these matters become issues that should concern leaders? When does the personal become professional?

Some leaders will find themselves in a situation where attitudes towards sensitive and controversial issues dealing with sex and sexuality have changed, but their own personal beliefs may or may not coincide with these changes. Equally, they could find themselves dealing with communities whose views toward issues such as single parenting, divorce, gays and lesbians are less enlightened than their own. Whose views should prevail? Are there absolute answers to these questions or do the answers change over time and from one culture to another? Training for leadership does not usually include exposure to matters involving sexuality but many school leaders find themselves having to address such issues.

Why it matters . . .

It is said that most people meet their partners at work. Relationships are likely to start (and finish) between teachers in the same school as in any other workplace.

As the *Times Educational Supplement Scotland* wrote in an editorial:

> Schools are natural locations for hormonal release. Lots of social interaction, lots of potential for relationships, lots of eyeing up, lots of actual getting it together . . . The reality is that staffrooms and classrooms are meeting places where fancies are stirred. There is always someone who is seeing someone, or would like to, and the high number of partners who stem from the same profession is testament to the success of the matching system. This runs right through education. But as we report elsewhere . . . matches can go awry. In confined workplaces that can lead to casualities.
>
> (TES Scotland, 2003, p. 12)

The editorial was referring to an article about a female teacher who alleged sexual harassment by her line manager. '*A Renfrewshire teacher has told an employment tribunal how her life was made hell at work by a ditched boyfriend who subsequently became her boss'* (Davidson, 2003, p. 6). The *Daily Record*'s coverage under the headline 'Teacher's pest fury' was fuller than that of the TES and reported intimate details of her complaints. (*Daily Record*, 2 August 2003).

These days all organisations have to consider issues such as sexual harassment and its consequences within and outside the institution. Some organisations also anticipate issues of *conflict of interest* when people are participating in a relationship, for example reducing the likelihood of a person receiving favourable treatment because of a relationship. School leaders are no different from leaders of any organisation in this respect. The particular additional issue for them is that they also have to think about the implications, if any, for their young charges – the pupils.

> In education, there is the additional pressure on teachers to conduct themselves morally not only for the sake of professionalism but also for the purpose of being moral exemplars to their own students . . . It further distinguishes teachers from lawyers, doctors, architects, accountants, engineers and other professionals who do not need to be concerned with modelling behaviour for the educative enrichment of their clients.
>
> (Campbell, 2003, p. 131)

Schools are expected to educate by example as well as by transmission. Education is deemed as more than attainment in exams.

> There is . . . a kind of moral fervour about the demands on schools to produce not only academically achieving young people, but also young people who are 'upright moral citizens', who refrain from taking drugs and from 'illicit' sexual practices . . . which brings sexuality strongly into the picture.
>
> (Epstein and Johnson, 1998, p. 6)

In addition to dealing with these situations as in any organisation, school leaders have to consider the reaction of the staff, the parents, the community and the potential consequences of unwelcome local and even national publicity.

Internal to the school

Sexual relations between members of staff in a school would generally be seen as their own business. However, even consensual sexual relations between two 'available' adults may have consequences for other people in the organisation. For example, there may be conflict of interest issues if a head of department responsible for performance management (or even the timetable) is having an affair with a member of his/her staff. There may also be issues of power and harassment to contend with in non-consensual relations such as line managers harassing staff they manage and staff harassing line managers. (This is not always 'top-down'. It is not unknown for female managers to be propositioned by male staff they manage).

There will be particular issues arising in some religious schools where leaders are expected to uphold a traditional moral stance that may, for example, not tolerate sexual relations between people who are not married to each other. These issues are discussed in more detail in the following chapters.

External to the school

Keeping on track with community

School leaders may find themselves dealing with a situation where the local community or small groups of the community hold discriminative views about sexuality, such as the parent who tried to 'out' a gay teacher discussed in chapter 2. Open enrolment means that the consequences of upsetting a considerable number of parents can be significant (e.g. they may decide to take their children out of the school, which in turn has consequences for funding). Keeping parents and the community on-side is not always easy. And then of course there is the possibility of the consequences of scandal particularly if the media is involved.

School sex stories and the media

Section 28

Sex sells and stories involving sex are frequently used by the media in a sensational way. Sex/sexuality and schooling seems to be of particular interest. This partly explains the difficulty the government had in attempting to repeal Section 28, legislation introduced by the

Conservative government in 1988 with the aim of preventing local authorities from intentionally promoting homosexuality and the teaching of homosexuality as a 'pretended family relationship' in maintained schools. (It was so named because it is Section 28 of the 1988 Local Government Act.) Section 28 was introduced by the Conservatives apparently to deal with so-called 'loony-left' local authorities that some people thought were encouraging young people to renounce heterosexuality for homosexuality. From January 2000 until September 2003 the Labour government tried to repeal it. The broadsheets were split on the question of whether this should happen. Headlines included 'Gay law row that ignited Middle England' (McSmith and Reeves, *Observer*, 30 January 2000, pp. 10–11) and in the same paper the leader's headline was 'Get a grip, Tony, knock 28 for 6'. On the same day the *Sunday Telegraph* led the front page with 'Blair is wrong over Section 28 says Woodhead' (Bentham, 2000). Chris Woodhead was at the time Her Majesty's Chief Inspector of Schools. Several features appeared following up the interim defeat of the campaign to repeal Section 28 describing experiences of gay and lesbian pupils in schools. One example was an article headed, 'I hated school. You have to put on an act every day' (Wallace, *Times Education Supplement*, 2000). When the House of Lords finally voted to repeal Section 28 in July 2003, (eventually ratified in September that year) one local education authority decided to reinstate its own version. The *Times Education Supplement* reported that:

> Tory-run Kent County Council has adopted its own version of Section 28 in anticipation of a repeal of the law banning local authorities from promoting homosexuality. It has brought in a new policy prohibiting the use of council tax-payers money for promoting homosexuality in its 600 schools.
>
> (Clark, 2003)

(Section 28 is discussed from a legal perspective in chapter 4.)

Any issue to do with gays and lesbians and schooling, appears to touch a particular nerve. (See, for example, Adler, 2000, for a description of the furore when the Inner London Education Authority included a book called *Jenny Lives with Eric and Martin* on a resource list; and Epstein and Johnson, 1998, for an analysis of the media's treatment of gay and lesbian issues in general.) Fear and fascination appear to be the most common dual reactions. The fear seems to be about homosexuality being contagious and the worry of corrupting young people by schools encouraging it as a 'normal practice'. The fascination for heterosexuals is about the unknown. These reactions make it much more difficult for school leaders to deal with such matters in a rational and ethical way.

Teachers behaving badly

All stories about schools and sex are bound to grab the headlines. Examples of 'teachers behaving badly', particularly with their pupils, are destined for the front page. This may be because teachers are supposed to behave in an exemplary manner themselves and impose good behaviour amongst their pupils. (The topic of teachers as role models is discussed further in chapter 2). In particular, teachers accused of having sex with pupils is virtually guaranteed to make headlines on national news. If the teachers are female, then international media interest is likely.

Two examples will suffice. The first case concerned a woman teacher in a private school accused of having sex with one of her 15-year-old male pupils. Broadsheet newspaper headlines included: 'Teacher admits she did strip in front of boys' (*Daily Telegraph*, 10 November 1999, p. 5); 'Woman teacher cleared of seducing pupil, 15' (*Daily Telegraph*, 11 November 1999, p. 1); and 'Revealed: sex case teacher's obsessive past'; 'Cleared teacher "was sexaholic"' (*Observer*, 14 November, 1999, pp. 1–2). (She was later cleared of the sex charge but dismissed for swimming in the nude in front of the boys.)

The second case concerned a Canadian teacher hired by a supply agency and undertaking short-term assignments in Surrey schools. She was charged with five counts of indecent assault against three of her male pupils. She was acquitted on all counts but it emerged during the trial that the police had investigated allegations about her having sex with a teenage pupil at a different school she had taught at in Surrey a few months previously. The boy at the first school was 16 (i.e. over age of consent) so no charges were brought because at the time she was not committing a criminal act (see chapter 4 for how this has since changed under the Sexual Offences Act, 2003). This happened even though the Child Protection Review Unit in Surrey had written to the supply agency warning them that she may pose a risk to children if she obtained another teaching position. The agency failed to heed this warning and did not pass the information on to the second school where they placed her. In this case, the tabloids reported in lurid detail the daily accounts of the schoolboy witnesses during the two-week trial. Most of the reporting in the broadsheets was about the way the supply agency had behaved and about the problem of tabloids paying witnesses for their story (possibly encouraging them to exaggerate), illustrated by the *Guardian*, 'Partying teacher casts a shadow over job agencies' and 'Move to outlaw witness payments' (5 February 2002, p. 4). Both the schools involved had to manage the considerable press, television and radio interest in the story. (Other cases involving female teachers are discussed in more detail in chapter 3.)

Deliberately, only quotations from broadsheets (so-called 'serious' press) have been used here. Any story that concerns sex and schooling is likely to attract a great deal of media coverage in the press and on television. As Epstein and Johnson (1998) have demonstrated, there are 'well established teacher and sexuality storylines in the tabloid press' (p. 94). In a context of 'parental choice' the sort of publicity that these stories produce is likely to affect enrolment; hence, most headteachers would prefer for them not to surface. However, many of these stories do reach the public arena and unprepared school leaders can be left to face a media circus. (See chapter 6 for advice about issuing press statements.)

In a profession like teaching, dealing with a perceived and/or potential scandal will not always bring out the most generous side of the community – local and professional. The profession may feel it has to exonerate itself and distance itself from the scandal. Rather than supporting those involved, it may close ranks and band together to blame and exclude them:

> The moral concern guides not just the response to risk but the basic faculty of perception. Compare, for example, the way that professions respond to the threat of scandal. The stronger the professional organization, the more it will insist on doing its own policing and punishing of its members, and the more strictly it will draw professional lines of accreditation and the more terrible the threat of disbarring a member at fault. The profession most deeply concerned with its collective reputation in the world of professions will be more inclined to protect its members and only to publicly criticize exemplary cases of misconduct when it can expel the defaulter.
>
> (Douglas, 1986, p. 60)

This may, of course, be a proper response to wrongdoers and a more appropriate one than covering up appalling errors such as those that came to light in the British health service (e.g. the low success rate of heart operations on babies undertaken at a Bristol hospital). These are the sort of issues now being dealt with by the teaching profession in the UK through the General Teaching Councils established in Scotland, Wales, Northern Ireland and England and discussed in more detail in chapter 5.

Avoiding scandal, or at least bad publicity, will be something most headteachers will strive to do. However tempting it is to keep these issues quiet, it is likely that at some time they will surface and need to be addressed. School leaders have always had to address issues of sexuality with the school (see, for example, Skidelsky cited later in this chapter), even though these can be the most difficult and the most sensitive they ever have to face, as in the past many leaders still prefer to brush them aside and pretend they do not exist.

Then and now

Not long ago, and even today in some religious schools and in some parts of the UK, sexual behaviour between unmarried adults was considered immoral. The discovery of any such behaviour would be deemed a matter for the headteacher to address. Women staff would invariably be asked to leave if they had a child out of wedlock. Indeed, until very recent times, women teachers were not officially allowed to have sex at all! If they did so when unmarried they were 'immoral' and if they got married they had to leave the profession anyway. The 'marriage bar' (for women teachers) in the UK was not finally lifted until 1944. (For more details of how the bar operated see Widdowson, 1980.)

Until the early part of the twentieth century it was assumed that women teachers should remain unmarried, partly in order to devote themselves fully to their jobs. The general consensus of opinion was that married women could not possibly cope with domestic and child rearing responsibilities and a professional job. However, changes in perception were under way and Oram (1996) charts how societal attitudes towards women teachers and their sexuality started to alter in this period. First, new ways of thinking prompted by the emergence of sexology and psychology as acceptable fields of study encouraged a reappraisal of the stereotype of the unmarried woman teacher:

Early twentieth century sexology and psychology meant that single women began to be seen as unfulfilled and sexually repressed while married women could be represented as truly womanly, and by extension, possibly better teachers than their unfortunate spinster colleagues.

(Oram, 1996, p. 185)

Second, there was a change in attitude and understanding of lesbianism, partly brought about by the publication in 1928 of Radclyffe Hall's novel *The Well of Loneliness*.

[this book] really marked a watershed in public awareness of lesbianism. This obscenity trial aroused a huge amount of publicity, and it has been argued that after this point, close friendships between women or adolescent girls were more closely scrutinised as potentially abnormal. There could be no more innocence about unmarried women.

(Oram, 1996, p. 188)

Consequently, single women teachers, who previously had been seen as a pure, positive and benevolent influence over young women, were now reconstructed as potentially damaging and possibly predatory.

Marie Stopes was concerned enough about this issue to write about the dangers lurking among an unmarried school staff:

There is increasingly the risk that there may be one or other member . . . who is partly or completely homosexual . . . it is not unknown (although it is generally hushed up) that such an individual may corrupt young pupils . . . Such perverts are not so rare as normal wholesome people would like to believe.

(Stopes, 1926, p. 53 quoted in Oram, 1996, p. 190)

The third change in public perception was that single women (single was equated with celibate) started to be seen as sexually repressed.

The women who have the responsibility of teaching these girls are many of them themselves embittered, sexless or homosexual hoydens who try to mould the girls into their own pattern. And far too often they succeed.

(Oram, 1996, p. 190, quoting from an address by
Dr Williams to an education conference in 1935
reported in the *Daily Herald*, 5 September, 1935.)

A. S. Neil who established Summerhill School describing 'a bad woman teacher', picked up this theme in his book *The Problem Teacher* published in 1939 by excusing her behaviour thus:

> In nine cases out of ten the poor woman is only acting as a sex-starved woman will act, and the cure for this type of teacher is manifestly a love life . . . It may be masculine arrogance on my part when I say that women teachers who have no sex life are more dangerous to children than men teachers in the same predicament . . . A system that puts the education of girls in the hands of a body of women who have no sex life is a mad one. It affords too much opportunity for jealousy. The homosexual woman does not want her girls to go on to heterosexuality.
>
> (Neil, 1939, pp. 63, 66, 97, 99, quoted in Oram, 1996, pp. 189–90)

According to Oram, during this period:

> There were three overlapping negative images of the single woman teacher: as an unfulfilled celibate and hence undesirable role model, as the predatory lesbian teacher, and as the militant feminist man-hating spinster.
>
> (Oram, 1996, p. 189)

Slowly attitudes changed until teaching came to be seen as a perfect occupation for married women with families. Women teachers were now allowed to have sex and children (as long as it was within marriage). Writing in 1957, Tropp suggested:

> Teaching, with its short hours, long holidays and opportunities for part-time work is the most convenient occupation for middle-class married women, and a teacher training is perhaps the most profitable investment for a girl whose aspirations include marriage and motherhood.
>
> (Tropp, 1957, p. 263)

Sexual behaviour may not have changed greatly over the years but what is considered *acceptable* sexual behaviour does shift over time and no doubt will continue to do so. Teachers about to retire will have seen many such changes during their careers. For example, societal attitudes have altered with regard to live-in partners, unmarried/sole parents, divorce and homosexuality.[1] Consequently, partly due to attitudinal changes in society, experienced headteachers may find themselves dealing very differently now, than they would have at the beginning of their career with issues relating to the private lives of their staff, e.g. 'living' together in common law relationships; staff who are unmarried parents (particularly women); or staff who are openly gay or lesbian.

Should headteachers 'keep up with the times' or should their values be constant and consistent over time? Does society expect headteachers of religious schools to behave differently from their secular counterparts? In particular how should all headteachers deal with sexual issues in an ever-changing context?

How does sexuality exist in schools?

These issues are not new. Any manifestation of sexuality has long been a concern of independent sector headteachers, particularly those of boys' boarding schools. Indeed, at least one head was encouraged to enter the profession in order to confront sexual misdemeanours. This was Reddie, the founding head of Abbotsholme School from 1889. He first turned to education because he believed that he had a mission to protect adolescents from sexual vice (Skidelsky, 1969). In the nineteenth century, apparently many public school headteachers went to great lengths to ensure that sexuality, especially homosexuality and masturbation had little chance of being practised in their boarding establishments:

> School authorities were adamant that there could be no tolerance of homosexual behaviour. Homosexuality was, they argued, highly contagious and only the expulsion of offenders from the school could protect other boys.
>
> (Hickson, 1995, p. 54)

Strategies used to prevent occurrence included cold showers, sewn-up pockets, spy-holes in study doors, doorless toilets, and severe rules about fraternising with older/younger boys and boys in other houses (Hickson, 1995). In order to uphold moral standards, headteachers even paid attention to the diet they provided for their pupils. Reddie was convinced that diet influences not only health, but also intellectual and moral stature. Meat stimulated the passions:

If boys at school are fed upon inflammatory food they are apt to lose control of themselves and have fits of irritability, leading very often to moral vice.

(Cecil Reddie, 1900, quoted in Skidelsky, 1969, p. 109)

In particular, special care was taken that no contact should take place at bedtime. A comparatively recent example cited by Hickson describing his own schooldays illustrates the point:

In the case of open-plan dormitories every pupil had his own clearly defined space with his chair and belongings on one side only of his bed. Each boy was forbidden from entering another's space and in the case of my own prep school, one frightened lad went down to the matron to ask permission to pick up his teddy which had fallen on the 'wrong side'.

(Hickson, 1995, p. 29)

In this time and context, headteachers were clear about their duties and responsibilities, even if according to survivors of these schools the strategies were often unsuccessful (Hickson, 1995).

At the beginning of the twenty-first century, the role of head-teachers and teachers (and others in authority over young people) in relation to sexuality issues is rather more ambiguous. As Wolpe points out, these issues can be embarrassing and it is often easier to pretend they do not exist. Nevertheless, she suggests that adults and pupils frequently relate to each other in a sexual way:

Sexuality spills over into the classroom and is one of the factors involved in the interchange between teachers and pupils.

(Wolpe, 1988, p. 129)

Even though sexuality may be 'spilling over into the classroom' these issues are rarely addressed directly in schools. As far as sexual behaviour between pupils is concerned:

Heterosexuality is the norm, and teachers presume that boy-friend and girlfriend liaisons will occur at school. But this is outside the bound of teachers' responsibilities, which, in the main, do not include concern with the sexuality of their pupils, particularly at the junior level of secondary school. In this way sex and sexuality may be largely ignored and teachers

are spared the uncomfortable need of having to deal formally
with adolescent sexual desires.

(Wolpe, 1988, p. 121)

Duncan agrees that teachers often ignore pupil sexuality but nevertheless sexual behaviour can have a profound impact on the way a
school operates:

> The disavowal of pupil sexuality enabled certain forms of
> discipline and control to function in the school's favour, but
> it still existed beneath almost every social exchange, ready to
> disrupt and distort honest relationships within the institution.
> (Duncan, 1999, p. 90)

It appears then that sex and sexuality are prevalent in schools, but
is this any business of school leaders?

The dilemma: when, if at all, should headteachers intervene?

> Schooling is in one sense a public activity, since it is carried
> on outside the home. But the school remains for the pupils a
> segregated setting distinct from the adult world of work and
> other involvement.
> (Giddens, 1991, p. 152)

Schools are complex organisations to manage. The public activity
of schooling is often manifested through essentially private encounters between pupils and their teachers. These private encounters
generally occur in classrooms behind closed doors. Even though
these encounters take place in the privacy of the classroom, they are
generally regarded as the legitimate business of school leaders and
those to whom they are accountable. Governments legislate or advise
on the curriculum and how it should be delivered. In the UK heads
are accountable for the quality of education in their schools.
So teachers are publicly accountable for an activity that takes place
in private. (Private does not mean *individual* and generally these
encounters are with groups of pupils.) Monitoring proceedings
behind closed doors has to be based on trust and a (usually
unwritten) agreement that certain behaviours are acceptable for a

teacher and others are not. What happens outside the classroom, in the public areas of the school, for example, in the corridors or staffroom or even in the vicinity of the school, is more complex. Some interactions such as a teacher speaking to a pupil in the corridor during the school lunch period, will be regarded by most as still within the boundaries of the teacher's professional remit and therefore could be the proper concern of the school leader. However, an encounter between two teachers at lunchtime could be viewed as purely personal and nothing to do with the headteacher. Alternatively, the head might take the view that anything that happens on school premises, whatever the time of day, is his/her legitimate business, but is it still their business if this lunchtime encounter takes place at the cafe next to the school or if the encounter takes place at the weekend? The point here is that there is a very fine line between private business and professional business. This is particularly true when issues of sexuality are involved.

> Sexuality: a subject which might seem a public irrelevance – an absorbing, but essentially private, concern . . . Yet in fact sex now continually features in the public domain.
>
> (Giddens, 1993, p. 1)

What are the boundaries? According to Giddens, 'There is no known culture in which sexual behaviour has been carried on in a completely open way under the gaze of everyone' (1991, p. 163). Sexual encounters are generally deemed to be private affairs but when does the private become professional?

When making a decision on these matters, school leaders may find the following criteria a useful start. The questions are from *The Ethical School*, by Felicity Haynes who suggests that educators should give consideration to the following three aspects of any situation:

- What are the consequences, both short and long term, for me and others, and do the benefits of any possible action outweigh the harmful effects?
- Are all the agents in this situation being consistent with their own past actions and beliefs? That is, are they acting according to an ethical principle/ethical principles that they would be willing to apply in any other similar situation? Are they doing to others as they would do unto them?

- Are they responding to the needs of others as human beings? Do they care about other people in this situation as persons with feelings like themselves?

(Haynes, 1998, pp. 28–29)

These issues are addressed in the next chapter.

Note

1   When I was teaching in a 'trendy' ILEA comprehensive in the early seventies, a single woman teacher who became pregnant was 'advised' to leave because of the (bad) example she would be setting to the pupils.

Chapter 2

Amongst equals? Teachers' sexual behaviour

Kate Myers

> Passion has become privatised; yet its implications and resonances are far from private.
>
> (Giddens, 1991, p. 205)

> Sexuality is . . . both inescapable and very dangerous territory for teachers. The tightrope which they have to walk between their public roles and private lives is one with an inbuilt insecurity.
>
> (Epstein and Johnson, 1998, p. 123)

> At one time teaching was regarded as a respectable profession, but its decline has been rapid and painful, no longer a career so much as an excuse for comedy.
>
> (*Time Out* reviewing Channel 4's television programme *Teachers*, TO no. 1725, pp. 160, 10–17, September 2003)

This chapter deals with sexual behaviour amongst adults involved in the school community. It raises issues about when, if at all, the sexual behaviour of staff is, or should be, the concern of school leaders. If a community expects its teachers to be model exemplars and upholders of moral virtues, there are obvious tensions if teachers then become involved in sexual behaviours that are deemed unacceptable and inappropriate. This of course raises the issue of what is inappropriate. For some communities, as discussed by Epstein and Johnson (1998), any sexual relationship that is not heterosexual and married would fall into this category.

Expectations of teachers' sexuality

As discussed in chapter 1, there is likely to be adverse reaction to any examples of teachers behaving badly. But what is improper or inappropriate behaviour for teachers as compared with the rest of the population?

In the nineteenth century there were very specific expectations of how teachers should dress and behave in and out of school. The managers of pupil teachers, for example, had to testify about the character of the pupil teacher and that of his, or her, parents.

> It was carefully ascertained whether the candidate lived under the 'constant influence of a good example' and if his family life did not bear scrutiny, he was to board in some approved household. 'Their Lordships' would not allow pupil-teachers to live in a public house, however well conducted it might be. Illegitimate children were not admitted, [into teaching] except in cases of outstanding merit, and even so they were required to move to some other place where they were not known.
>
> (Tropp, 1957, p. 22)

So, in the nineteenth century, it was expected that teachers should not be illegitimate (unless they were exceptional) nor have overt connections with public houses. Other expectations were often based on gender, reflecting prevailing views about the place of women in society. These views started to change in the twentieth century. The lifting of the marriage bar in 1944 acknowledged that women could both teach and be married. (This was never deemed a conflict for male teachers.) While the marriage bar was in force:

> The only means of enjoying a heterosexual relationship while keeping a teaching post [for women teachers] was either to marry secretly or cohabit secretly with a male partner. Either option carried many risks . . . 'Living together' was morally unacceptable and would bring instant dismissal if revealed, as would concealment of marriage.
>
> (Oram, 1996, p. 56)

As one London teacher, talking about living with her partner before marriage, in the interwar years, said, 'The phrase "living in sin", it really meant that, and as you were sinful you weren't the right sort to have anything to do with children, so you both would have lost [teaching] Certificates' (Oram, 1996 pp. 56–7).

In the UK, until the latter part of the twentieth century there appeared to be general consensus about the way teachers were supposed to behave. It was presumed that they would reflect the traditional and pervading mores of society. When they 'broke the rules' there were sanctions including that of dismissal. As these traditional attitudes (e.g. towards marriage, divorce and illegitimacy) started to change it became more difficult to be certain about the role model that should be adhered to by teachers – and headteachers.

Some school leaders and some school communities still have strong views about what role models they want and expect. Consequently, what is considered appropriate dress and behaviour for staff is overt and adhered to. According to the Association of Teachers and Lecturer's (ATL) solicitor, Philip Lott, an employer can enforce a dress code and if the governors decided to do this, teachers would have to conform to it 'provided it is carefully and sympathetically applied with regard to race discrimination rules' (Lott, 1996). Many schools however, adopt a more *laissez-faire* approach and address these issues as they arise, for example, if in their view a member of staff is dressed inappropriately for work. In some cases policies have been developed that directly address the issue of teacher behaviour with pupils in school (see chapter 6 for examples) and since 2003, 'beginning teachers' have had to show that '*They demonstrate* and promote the positive values, attitudes and behaviour that they expect from their pupils' (TTA, 2003, para 1.3, p. 3, my italics). (This requirement is somewhat vague and it will be interesting to see what evidence is necessary to show that the criteria have been reached.)

According to Haydon, writing in 1997, 'Teachers are still regarded as moral guides and exemplars, whose standards are perhaps just a little above the level of the rest of society' (pp. 4–5). This is no doubt true in some parts of the world and some parts of the UK but the stereotype of the upright teacher may be changing. Channel 4's *Teachers* programme, for example, reveals a totally different image of teachers. This light hearted drama series focuses on the social and sexual aspects of its characters' lives rather than the professional. The teachers in the series are portrayed as degenerate and irresponsible rather than moral exemplars. There are objections to showing teachers in this way (see chapter 5) particularly by those who believe that such images affect public perceptions of the profession. If the profession want to reclaim the image of 'teacher as moral guide and exemplar' then what is considered inappropriate behaviour and how misdemeanours are dealt with, becomes particularly important.

Behaviour outside of school

If society does see teachers and headteachers as role models and moral exemplars, the expectations do not stop at the end of the school day. There are implications for their behaviour outside of the confines of the school building and school hours. For example, Piddocke *et al.* (1997) quote a 1987 case in British Columbia, Canada, where a teacher was suspended because her husband submitted a semi-nude photograph of her to a photographic magazine and it was subsequently published. She was suspended on the grounds that:

> Teachers are expected to be role models for their students and that this role includes upholding the values of the community outside the classroom as well as in it.
>
> (p. 115)

Young teachers entering the profession at the beginning of the twenty-first century will have been students at a time when taking 'recreational drugs' was considered acceptable practice amongst many of their peers. Some of those who took drugs as students will stop as soon as they become teachers. Others may continue. It is clear that any member of staff caught under the influence of drugs (or alcohol) on the school premises would be subject to disciplinary procedure (and possibly legal sanctions). It is less clear what happens if they indulge in this habit out of school hours though presumably certain factors such as whether they were likely to be seen by pupils, what sort of drug etc. was involved would be taken into account.

As Graham Clayton and David James both say later in this book, there is no commonly agreed definition of 'teachers behaving badly'. School leaders have to decide whether the behaviour in question has an adverse effect on the school and whether it results in being unable to trust the teacher to carry out their school duties.

In the mid-1990s in an inner-city school, a teacher was caught with ecstasy tablets in her possession at the weekend. She admitted that she took ecstasy when 'clubbing'. The teacher's explanation was that she regularly went out with the same group of friends. They each took their turn to obtain the drug for the group before attending a rave. It was her turn when she was stopped and searched by the police as she entered the rave. Because she was found to have four tablets in her possession she was charged with intent to supply drugs to others, a far more serious offence than being in possession of the drug for her own use. She immediately informed her headteacher of her arrest and the nature of the charge.

This is the head's story.

I wished to be as supportive as possible of a valued, if misguided colleague, who had a previously unblemished record and was well regarded by students, parents and colleagues. I immediately consulted the chair of governors. Their dilemma was that the teacher was charged with a criminal act that could, at worst, lead to a custodial sentence. At the very least she would be seen by most parents and many, if not all, of her professional colleagues to be an unacceptable role model for students. Additionally, the school would be vulnerable to extensive and widespread criticism from every quarter, but especially the popular press if it did not take action.

With the support of the chair of governors, I chose not to act immediately, but waited to see how the situation might develop. Some weeks later the teacher was summonsed to appear in court. Her solicitor warned her that she might be given a custodial sentence. At that stage she decided to plead guilty to the charge of 'supply' in order to curtail the proceedings and to avoid the complications of a prolonged hearing, which might also involve her friends. It was also likely that the case might attract the attention of the press and if so, the matter would inevitably become public. The school would then be open to criticism for not taking prior action against the teacher.

One week before the trial I decided that there was no alternative, but to suspend the teacher. My sympathy and support for a colleague were outweighed by a much greater responsibility for the reputation of the school. This decision was accepted and understood by the teacher and her union representative. However, the shorter period of absence from school was much easier to manage for the school and for the teacher. After a brief hearing she was found guilty as charged, but after taking account of her previous record of good behaviour and excellent character references from well-regarded members of her community, including me, the judge sentenced her to a period of community service.

The subsequent meeting of the disciplinary committee of the school's governors found her guilty of serious misconduct, but chose only to severely reprimand her. Subsequently the teacher has continued to fulfil her responsibilities effectively, but her concern about the difficulties of revealing this matter to a prospective employer has, to date, discouraged the teacher from applying for promotion that is well within her capacity. However, an effective teacher has at least been able to continue in her current post. This might not have been possible if her case had attracted the publicity that had originally been anticipated.

(Anonymous submission)

We know from the response to any incident of teachers behaving badly, that certain standards are expected by the general public, but exactly what these standards are in the early twenty-first century is not always obvious and consequently can be quite a difficult issue for school leaders to address. (Some advice is offered in the second half of this book). The scenario illustrates how much these issues are in the hands of individual headteachers. A head who held strong anti-drugs views is likely to have taken a different stance from the one above. Because of the consequences of unwelcome publicity heads tend to be cautious in these matters as the following advice shows.

Convictions or cautions for possession of cannabis can present governors with a quandary. While some may personally take the view that cannabis is harmless, they need to recognise that society is sharply divided on the issue and that, in child protection terms, employees who use drugs are seen as a risk to children. Therefore, governors should think carefully about appointing people with recent convictions or cautions for possessing drugs, especially to posts where they would have an influence on children and young people. As a rough rule of thumb, they should avoid employing anyone who committed a drug-related offence while employed in the education service.

(Cooper and Curtis, 2000, p. 17)

Teachers' sexual behaviour

When situations involving 'inappropriate' sexual behaviour are brought to the attention of the head, s/he usually has little choice but to at least address the matter and, in some cases, intervene. An example where intervention would be expected is the discovery of a member of staff having a sexual relationship with a pupil in their care, but other examples (for instance, consensual sexual relations between adults in the school) may not be quite as clear-cut. Such consensual relationships between teachers do at times present issues for the head. It is said that most adults meet their partners at work. This is likely to be particularly true of jobs that require long hours when this means that people do not get much time, nor do they have a lot of energy, to socialise elsewhere. The notion may well bring a wry smile to the lips of heterosexual teachers who work in the same-sex environment (or predominantly the same) such as primary and many special schools. Nevertheless, in many primary and special and most large secondary schools there is ample opportunity for relationships between teachers (and between teachers and other adults in the school) to start – and finish – in the workplace, as discussed in chapter 1.

Many such relationships have happy endings but this does not always happen and can create difficult situations for the protagonists and their colleagues. According to one history teacher in a large comprehensive school:

> 'When X started working at my school, I fancied her straight . . . She was great fun, very sociable, but also committed to her job. As a newly qualified teacher, she was obviously under pressure, but we became close friends and started going out together a few months later.' Initially, they were secretive about

their relationship, but when they went public, things began to deteriorate . . . What he wasn't prepared for was her reaction to being dumped. 'She didn't care who knew how upset she was . . . There were tears and tantrums in the staffroom, notes left on my car and in my register where anyone could have seen them – even the students. It was very embarrassing.'

(Murray, 2004, p. 1)

In this particular case a senior member of staff spoke to the teacher concerned and she changed her behaviour; however the history teacher said 'It's been a few years now, but things are still awkward between us. For me, dating a colleague was a big mistake. I wouldn't be keen to repeat the experience' (Murray, 2004, p. 1). Nevertheless, in the same article in spite of these concerns, Susan Quilliam, a relationship psychologist, is quoted as saying 'teaching isn't like any other job. . . . Many teachers find that partners from other professions don't understand the pressures they are under. And many are so busy at work they simply don't get the opportunity to meet people' (Murray, 2004, p. 1). Sexual relationships between staff become inevitable in such circumstances as many school leaders have discovered when they are asked to address the consequences.

One example is the head of a large comprehensive who was faced with a staff delegation asking her to take action with regard to an ongoing relationship between two teachers.

A group of staff asked to see me. They said they were acting on behalf of what they described as a 'large number of colleagues'. This vague statement was backed up by a letter signed by about 30 out of 100 staff. It included a number of those in middle management positions. They said they were extremely upset and concerned about X – a young woman head of department whose husband, also on the staff, had left her for XX, one of our heads of year.

I listened carefully to the delegation. It was clear that they wanted me to take action against the husband. I told them that as headteacher, I was naturally concerned about the well-being of all the staff. However it was not possible to make judgements without knowing both sides and the full circumstances. In the circumstances I counselled all those who had come to see me to consider the situation very carefully and if there was one of them who felt they had never done anything that might have hurt another I would willingly see them to discuss this further.

There was not an issue of neglect of duties by any of the people concerned but I realised it must have been very difficult for the woman who had been deserted and of course it was of concern to me that a member of staff was unhappy. Through my senior team we did make sure that she was supported as much as we could. We were also concerned that the status of the head of year was not put in jeopardy. It certainly was an undermining situation for her. The man who had left his wife did find that his status was negatively affected within the school.

As time went by the young head of department left for a promotion to another school. The new couple settled down and worked hard. It is now all considered water under the bridge.

(Anonymous submission)

If two members of staff start 'dating' it could be argued that this is no one's business but theirs. The people concerned in the relationship may wish to keep it private. In the early days, one or both of them may not even be sure that there is anything to declare (literally because of conflicts of interest – as discussed in Chapter 1 and Chapter 6 – or metaphorically because at the very beginning they do not want everyone to know). For those who have no wish to remain discrete, headteachers may have to decide whether holding hands or kissing in front of colleagues or pupils is appropriate behaviour on the school premises – or even in the vicinity of the school.

Playing tonsil tennis in the high street or the back row of the cinema is definitely out – particularly if you live and work in the same town. But even if you are discreet, the very idea of a teacher dating a colleague can be intriguing for your pupils. [The wife of one couple now married explained] 'As soon as we met, we really hit it off . . . But staff relationships seemed to be frowned upon, so it took us a year or so to get together. As soon as we did, the rumour machine was under way. We tried to be discreet, but were soon spotted out together by students and then the gossip started. At first it was quite amusing, but then it became upsetting. Because John had been married before and had a child at the school, the students were saying we'd had an affair and I'd broken up the marriage. I know it was only student gossip, but I hated to think what they were going home and telling their parents . . . You have to remember that teenagers are just coming to terms with love and sex . . . So if "Sir" starts dating "Miss", they are going to find out'.

(Murray, 2004, p. 1)

School leaders may have to intervene in such scenarios before gossip reaches the governors or indeed the local press. They may also have to decide whether or not the same protocol exists for gay and lesbian couples.

The scenario may get more complex if, for example:

- One or both of the teachers are married to someone else (or deemed to be 'attached') as a previous and following scenarios illustrate.

> When I was deputy head of a primary school I became increasingly aware of the growing relationship between two teachers and knew that gossip was also developing. I believed the head had not noticed as it had certainly not been spoken about. I knew the spouse of one of the teachers who worked in another school close by. As the affair seemed to be gathering momentum I felt something had to be done and asked to see them together – although in the days, hours and minutes before the meeting I felt physically sick at the thought. The thought entered my head that I might be wrong and even if I was right did it overstretch my role in the school to

interfere in this way. It was only the thought of repercussions should children and parents begin to notice the situation that made me tackle it at all. I made it clear that it had only become my business because they were becoming the subject of staffroom gossip, and asked that they contained their obvious feelings for each other to private moments away from the school premises. Although clearly embarrassed, they saw the point and agreed to do as I requested. Relationships were a little strained as a result but the situation was contained and did not ultimately affect their careers or the children. The affair eventually fizzled out and as far as I am aware one marriage did break down eventually but the other is still secure.

(Anonymous submission)

Additional scenarios to be considered are:

- A teacher is involved in sexual relationships with more than one colleague
- A teacher embarks on an affair with a married parent or school governor
- An 'available' parent or governor has an affair with a married teacher.

Some would argue that because of possible repercussions for the school, all these scenarios could be considered the business of the head. One extreme example occurred in a West Sussex Comprehensive school in 2001 where Mark Parnham and his wife Jillian taught. When he discovered that she was having an affair with another teacher in the school he bludgeoned her to death with a metal bar (from the school). He was acquitted of murder but found guilty of manslaughter and sentenced to six years in jail (Hendrie, 2002). He subsequently became the first teacher to be struck off the teaching register by the General Teaching Council in March 2003 (Abrams, 2003, p. 8).

Less extreme scenarios can still be problematic for school leaders as the following illustration from a primary head suggests:

Two members of my primary team started a relationship. The young woman was, I think it would be fair to say, considerably less worldly wise than the young male teacher. She was also less experienced as a teacher, less aware of social issues in her classroom, and her actual knowledge and understanding of the curriculum was weaker. So in many ways the relationship benefited not just her, but our school. While she was in this relationship, there was a noticeable improvement in the depth of her planning and ability to see connections and not just teach to the rule book. This matters in a primary school, where strict adherence to the letter of the Strategies can result in very desiccated classroom practice.

After about six months, the relationship broke up. The young woman suffered considerable emotional distress. In fact she took several weeks off school and I was concerned about her level of depression. She had confided in me, as head, that she and the male teacher 'were seeing each other' to use her own rather old-fashioned phrase, and I also knew when the relationship ended.

Both these teachers are still on my staff. It is difficult to know how to support her.

(Anonymous submission)

Heads may also be confronted with ethical dilemmas that are tangential to the behaviour in question. For example, given a teacher 'behaving badly' it might be tempting to deal differently with a highly effective teacher compared with one that is not, and particularly one that the head would love to leave the school. One head found:

Encountering the deputy head in flagrante delicto with the school secretary – the former being male, the latter female – was not in my rule book. I didn't know what to do. The event occurred in his office, 'out of school time' – as he later commented. Having initially knocked on his door, before entering, I was shocked by the sight of flailing female legs, tights at half mast, and when she emerged from under his unmistakable bulk, I saw my recently appointed secretary. I choose the word 'shocked' with care. Not until later did the word carry moral meaning, the first impact was shock, as in 'shock and awe'.

I had been in the headship job for a few months and was already aware that this deputy thought I needed challenging. He was older and more experienced than me and his particular skills lay in controlling pupils and exerting his own kind of power over staff. He was invariably off-site at lunchtime. He was clearly scornful of efforts to broaden the school's intake to a more demanding mix, socially and academically.

Thus my observing of his more carnal tendencies was part of a larger set of concerns. I discussed the matter with the local authority adviser and he doubted it was a clear-cut disciplinary case. I later learnt that in that local authority at that time, there was virtually nothing that counted as a 'clear-cut disciplinary case'. That was the climate then.

With the chair of governors, I proceeded to discuss the incident with the deputy head and followed it through with a written note. This wasn't a correct procedure, but I couldn't simply ignore it. Three years later he took early retirement, but a lot of harm had been done to the school in the meantime.

(Anonymous submission)

Even if both adults were 'available' and competent in their work it could be that the relationship is not consensual; one person could be pursuing the other without their feelings being reciprocated. When issues of power are involved, as when an older and/or more senior member of staff pursues someone younger, it is not too difficult to see the possibility of sexual harassment emerging, as illustrated in the following vignette:

I worked in a school where an older, married teacher would press himself up against me at the office filing cabinet, under the pretence of offering help. At an office party I found out he was doing this to all the young women teachers, so I put a note on the filing cabinet saying: 'Don't do any filing if you are alone in the room with (this man). He'll treat you like his personal property.' He was so embarrassed that he stopped immediately. We could have gone to the headmaster, but the note was so effective we didn't need to make a fuss.

(Williams, 2000, p. 7)

Given the mores of our society, this scenario is most likely to be male to female but it can happen, female to male. It is also important to remember that power does not always reside with the person with the senior status. Hence, managers can be sexually (and racially) harassed by their staff, and teachers can be harassed by their pupils.

Less extreme, but nevertheless tricky scenarios to deal with, include situations such as the following:

When I was deputy head of a primary school one of my female colleagues went through a messy divorce. Her reaction was to go on a sexual razzmatazz. She started to wear clothes that in my view were inappropriate for work – see-through blouses with plunging necklines, extremely skimpy skirts which revealed more than they should as she bent over her small pupils. She seemed to sleep with a different man virtually every night and would come into school and recall her encounters in vivid detail in the staff room. She had always been a 'plan the day on the bus' kind of teacher, and her late nights at whatever club she was frequenting didn't help her planning or her class teaching. Nevertheless, as senior managers, the head and I really didn't know how to handle this situation. I for one was not happy about the sexist responses from the male head about her behaviour – for example, that she was 'anybody's'. So, though I think she was probably stretching professional limits – I felt I might be colluding with his judgemental, insulting sexism if I agreed to take things up with her. In any event, I really wasn't sure how much what was going on out of school was our business.

(Anonymous submission)

With regard to sexual behaviour, heads are not always the role models society expects. What should the head do if he or she is having a relationship with a member of staff or a governor? At what point should there be a public declaration of interest?

This is one head's story of what happened when he fell in love with his deputy.

My wife and I met when she was appointed as deputy in the school where I was head. Some six months after her appointment we fell in love. At the time we were both married to other people and seen as married by the 'outside' world (including colleagues at school). The fact that we were in relationships that had effectively ended was clearly a private matter and could not be discussed by any but the most intimate of friends. All this meant that our relationship started secretly. This had significant implications for us personally and professionally – and in many ways the two overlapped. On the personal side we were conducting an 'affair', with all the excitement, tension and guilt that that generates. Our professional lives increased the need for such secrecy. We had to make sure that we were not seen as a couple by members of the school community – staff, students and parents and even by friends. We did though, tell governors and the director of education about six months on – once we were sure the relationship was long-term.

In connection with our work, we very early agreed we would not discuss anything that might compromise our professional relationships with colleagues. For example, we would not go over SMT agendas with each other outside of school nor would we discuss particular issues or staff we might be dealing with at the time. Initially, such caution was probably motivated as much by the need to keep the relationship secret as by our concept of professionalism. However, although we didn't know it then, we were laying the groundwork for the time when we went public.

The 'outing' came with both our divorces and, after a period, we started living together openly prior to getting married. At this point things in school changed. Whereas before we were the only two who understood the potential dangers of talking through work issues at home, now there were colleagues (particularly senior colleagues) who, if they were not actually looking for breaches of professionalism, were aware that they could happen. We decided we needed to share, with staff, our understanding of the responsibility we felt to keep school completely out of our home lives. We wanted to be sure that no one would be able to say that we had, for example, agreed a line on a contentious issue or had passed on to each other something said in confidence by another member of staff. Although we loved working together (and the delight in that experience was a major factor in our eventual marriage) we didn't always agree and there were numerous occasions in SMT meetings where the vigour and freshness of our exchanges left no one in any doubt that there had not been prior collusion!

Only one colleague appeared to have a problem with our relationship. Someone leaked a story to the local press to the effect that the head's relationship with his deputy was a major factor in her getting a pay rise. The story that might have seriously damaged both of us, however, was completely turned round when staff circulated a statement to the effect that they had total confidence in our integrity. Only one member failed to sign it!

Our successful attempts at separating the private and the professional meant that, when they arose, tricky issues regarding other staff relationships were easier to deal with. For example, once we had to suggest to a member of staff who was still seen as married by the parent and student population that sharing a tent on a school residential with his new-found partner, a colleague from another department, was not a good idea! The prompting was responded to positively.

> Schools are full of relationships which start in the schools themselves – probably because of the intensity of the work and the need to support, and be supported by, trusted colleagues. Our own previous marriages started with relationships in previous schools. The school I have been referring to generated at least another four serious long-term relationships.
>
> (Anonymous submission)

However, not all relationships will be as serious or long term as the one described above. 'Lothario' headteachers exist, though when 'outed' may not be deemed by many governing boards to fulfil the necessary role model image of headteachers, particularly in faith schools. A short piece in the *Times Educational Supplement* (*TES*) under the headline 'Affairs head quits family school' read:

> The head of a top church school has resigned after admitting a string of affairs. [name] stunned parents at . . . Church of England School . . . with a letter in which he confessed to 'extramarital relationships'. Last week he resigned from the school, which prides itself on its 'family environment', the diocese of . . . said.
>
> (*TES*, 23 November 2001, p. 4)

Of course, none of the scenarios previously described are restricted to heterosexuals, and all could be between gay men or between lesbians. Gay and lesbian teachers often find it very difficult to 'come out' and feel they have to live a life of deceit. For example, it can be difficult for them to participate easily in staffroom banter about partners or domestic life. Those who prefer to keep their sexuality private may be vulnerable to being 'outed' by colleagues, pupils, parents or governors. Sometimes the consequences for individuals, and even a school, can result in adverse publicity and be devastating for those involved. The ethos that a head seeks to create will have an effect on how supported gay and lesbian teachers feel.

Epstein and Johnson (1998) discuss the case of a teacher called Neil, for whom a visit to a friend known to be gay was observed by a mother of a pupil in the school in which Neil taught. The mother started making allegations about Neil: 'The head reacted against the mother's homophobic abuse. She was not prepared to condone this overt bigotry' (p. 138).

However:

> Although she was ready to stand against overt homophobia, she had little grasp of the everyday lives of lesbian and gay teachers or of the risks to them as a result of being outed through chance circumstances or of the more pervasive character of sexual gossip about teachers generally.
>
> (p. 139)

Uninformed concern about HIV and AIDS has also made the life of some gay teachers virtually unbearable, as described in the following extract:

> Having been revealed as a homosexual during a protracted period of absence from school, he found that on his return he was the brunt of colleagues' fears about AIDS and that he was precluded from effectively discharging his duties as a deputy head.
>
> (Squirrell, 1989, p. 23)

Squirrell goes on to describe how this teacher was isolated, his head refused to work with him, teachers left the staffroom when he entered and he was forced to take lunch on his own. The supply teacher covering his class refused to do so until the room had been 'scrubbed out'. Squirrell offers other examples on the same theme:

> In one London school two openly gay teachers have been ostracised with colleagues refusing to use the same toilets or even coffee mugs. Teachers who are, or are suspected of being gay are suffering increased harassment from both pupils and colleagues.
>
> (London Gay Teachers group, 1985,
> quoted in Squirrell, 1989)

School leaders need to be aware that since the Employment Equality (Sexual Orientation Regulations) which came into effect in December 2003, such behaviour could end up in the courts. Since this regulation came into effect:

> Discrimination on grounds of sexual orientation (or a presumed orientation) [is outlawed] towards persons of the same sex, opposite sex or towards both. The legislation covers gays, lesbians, heterosexuals and bisexuals . . . Transgender people are protected by separate regulations . . . Harassment on grounds of sexual orientation is specifically unlawful. And harassment covers unwanted conduct violating a person's dignity or creating an intimidating, hostile, degrading, humiliating or offensive environment.
>
> (Pilkington, 2004, p. 20)

Heads have to deal with the implications of their own sexuality as well as that of the people they manage. If headteachers themselves are gay or lesbian, their decision about whether to keep this private or not can be a very difficult one to make (see MacBeath and Myers, 1999). Being open with colleagues is not always possible, for example, when the relationship is same-sex and those involved do not want to declare their sexuality.

Other facets of sexuality that heads may also have to address in their professional capacity include transvestism and transsexuality. According to Piddocke *et al.* (1997, p. 151), transvestism is where a member of one sex dresses as a member of the other sex and transsexuality is where a member of one sex tries to change his/her body until it fits the bodily form of the other sex. The authors quote a 1979 case in Alberta, Canada, where a teacher was dismissed for stealing women's clothes. The school board justified his sacking on two grounds. First, because he had pleaded guilty to the charge of stealing and second because:

> He had manifested abnormal behaviour, which included storing women's clothing and accessories in his classroom and wearing women's clothes in the school building, albeit during off-hours when the building was closed to the public . . . He was discovered on two occasions cross-dressing in the school. After the first incident, he was met with sympathy by school authorities and directed to take special counselling, which he did. Some time later, however, 'the stolen property was discovered in the school, the situation became general knowledge in the . . . district and obviously the Respondent was obligated by public pressure to deal with the question.' Mr A. was first suspended and then dismissed.
>
> (Piddocke *et al.*, 1997, p. 151)

In the UK there have been recent reported incidents of teachers changing their sex and in some cases returning to their school with a different identity. For example:

> '*Catholic head backs sex change*'. The headteacher of a Roman Catholic school is supporting a female teacher who is undergoing a sex change. Parents of children at the . . . have been informed that technology teacher Mrs LA will be known as Mr SA from Monday. A letter to parents from headteacher JM said that assemblies have been arranged this week to help youngsters understand 'the unusual circumstances'.
>
> (*TES*, 3 March 2000, p. 8)

The names of the school and person concerned were reported in full in this short news item. (It is noteworthy that the empathetic response to this teacher occurred in a faith school.) Later in the same month, in the *TES*'s question and answer page for school managers, an anonymous head asked for help. S/he wrote:

> It has come to my attention as head that a member of staff is starting the process of a sex change. She has not told me of this, but pupils and colleagues are already noticing changes in her physical appearance and dress. What should I do?
>
> (*TES*, 24 March 2000, p. 27)

The following year, the main headline on the front page of the TES read 'Sex-change teacher in rights fight' (5 October 2001, p. 1). The article, below a large picture of 'Natasha . . . a transsexual teacher', described how she had just won almost £4,000 in compensation after 'an East Sussex primary [school] accepted it had discriminated against her' (p. 1).

As Epstein and Johnston (1998) suggested at the beginning of this chapter the tightrope which teachers have to walk between their public roles and private lives can be very difficult, particularly when issues of sex and sexuality are concerned. The dilemma school leaders face is keeping on the right side of the boundary between other people's business (that is none of theirs) and making decisions about when intervention is proper and appropriate because of the (possible) impact on the school. There are no easy answers to these dilemmas. They concern moral and ethical principles and need to be addressed with sensitivity and wisdom.

Although this chapter has dwelt on issues concerning teaching staff, other adults who have contact with pupils are also the responsibility of the head, in particular, support staff (e.g. administrators, classroom assistants, learning and behaviour mentors, caretakers, technicians, librarians, cooks, cleaners). All the scenarios described above can affect them too. Because of power and status issues some support staff will be more vulnerable to sexual harassment than other workers in the school. When the person being harassed belongs to a minority ethnic group, racial stereotypes compound the sexual ones and they are vulnerable to being targets of both sexual and racial discrimination.

This chapter has raised issues about the sexual behaviour between teachers and between teachers and other adults linked with the school. The following chapter explores issues to do with teachers and their pupils.

Chapter 3

The age of innocence?
Pupils and teachers

Kate Myers

> One of the greatest betrayals of students by a teacher or admin-
> istrator is that of sexual harassment, assault, abuse or rape. Despite
> the outrageousness of such behaviours, they are not uncommon.
>
> (Curcio *et al.*, 1996, p. 38)

> There is an increased sophistication in the sexual knowledge
> of children and young people, with television in particular
> making accessible to children the secrets that adults used to keep
> to themselves . . . children nowadays are encouraged to present
> themselves as sexual beings at an ever younger (and thus arguably
> more vulnerable) age.
>
> (Halstead and Reiss, 2003, p. 19)

> We may assume that because of their age, education, maturity,
> experience, authority, and status, teachers always hold the power
> in teacher-student relationships. However, teachers also report
> being embarrassed, degraded, undermined, and humiliated by
> students. In most cases, the victims are female teachers.
>
> (Shoop and Edwards, 1994, quoted in Curcio *et al.*, 1996, p. 37)

Sexual behaviour that occurs between adults in the school has been
discussed in the previous chapter. Here the focus is about sexual
behaviour between teachers and pupils including flirting as well as
more serious offences. Incidents may not be an everyday occurrence
in most schools but they do occur:

> In one Midlands secondary over a 10-year period there were
> three cases of staff having unsuitable relationships with pupils.
> One woman was dismissed after a police prosecution. A music

teacher resigned after a relationship with a 15-year-old pupil came to light and a science teacher was given an informal warning after he was accused of inappropriate behaviour.

Projected nationwide, that school's experience suggests that 1,500 teachers a year are involved in relationships with pupils. These cases remain buried for one simple reason. Everyone concerned – school, parents and teacher – is keen to avoid the limelight. There is often no formal complaint and sometimes no evidence of any wrongdoing – just a suspicion.

(Revell, 2002, p. 1)

Flirting and untargeted sexual behaviour

Many men and women relate to each other in a sexual or gendered way as a matter of course and teachers are no different here. This behaviour is part of their 'social script'. The script is employed (often unwittingly) in order to interact with other people in day to day situations that do not necessarily have sexual connotations.

For both sexes, flirting is an example of using sexual behaviour in daily interactions. Flirting here is defined as 'behav[ing] in a frivolously amorous or sexually enticing manner' (*Oxford Dictionary*, 1991). More often than not, this behaviour is employed when serious sexual entanglement is not envisaged by either party. When consensual and welcomed it can be harmless and the way many adults choose to interact with each other. Flirting becomes problematic when it is not consensual and when issues of power are involved, for example, when teachers flirt with pupils. Wolpe (1988) observed that in some schools and with some teachers, sexuality is used as a (unacknowledged and usually unconscious) method of control:

> the interpersonal relationships between staff and pupils in which teachers unconsciously employ sexual ploys in order to aid them in the control over pupils . . . The pupils would not consciously recognize what was happening in the classroom. But this constitutes part of the 'social scripting'.
>
> (pp. 141–2)

Wolpe believed that one of her male teacher interviewee's thought that:

mild flirtation between the male teachers and the older girls was good for both of them. He suggested that this would help keep the girls interested in school and prevent them from going 'wild' in the course of seeking pleasure outside of the school. Here [compounding racism with sexism] he suggested that the problems were particularly acute with 'West Indian' girls.

(1988, pp. 129–30)

Flirting may be linked to the age and stage (in career) of the teacher concerned as well as that of the pupil(s). For example, a male teacher may find it 'natural' to interact with young women pupils by flirting with them and thus see no harm in this sort of behaviour. Indeed it may be the way such an individual has 'learnt' to interact with all women:

> Male teachers were quite open about their attitudes towards the girls, often putting their arms around the girls, and making comments such as, 'You're looking gorgeous today'.
>
> (Jones, 1985, p. 29)

New technologies have increased the opportunities for flirting. For example, inappropriate texting and emailing between teachers and their pupils has been cited as a concern by the General Teaching Council's disciplinary panel (see chapters 5 and 6).

Much sexual banter and sexual behaviour will be considered harmless by many. However, as attitudes to different kinds of sexuality have changed, so too have attitudes in some quarters about what is considered sexist and inappropriate sexual behaviour. Heads have to help the school community decide at what point harmless innuendo becomes harmful sexual harassment or even abuse.

For some people, behaving in a traditional masculine or feminine way is part of their normal demeanour. For some teachers these behaviours can be a significant part of the repertoire they use for controlling pupils.

> The pervasiveness of certain forms of masculinity as a means of controlling boys in school create unintended and perhaps unnoticed consequences. . . . some male teachers still used heavy physical contact with some types of unruly boys in an informal, jokey way to control their classroom behaviour. Other practices included the articulation of masculine interests of domination,

partisan support for the group, and heterosexuality in an inter-generational, cross-class discourse of male solidarity. Those teachers' survival techniques were never acknowledged as a form of sexual bullying, but essentially that is what they were.

(Duncan, 1999, p. 125)

The messages these interactions display are picked up by pupils as Duncan, observed in a school in the West Midlands:

The highly gendered interactions between male staff . . . appealed to many of the boys witnessing them. Physically powerful, authoritative and noble, the masculinity dominant in these images was digested by the pupil culture and its forms replayed in general social relations.

(Duncan, 1999, p. 121)

This type of behaviour is generally the prerogative of male teachers. Women would find it very difficult, if not impossible, to include such strategies in their repertoire. They also often find it difficult to deal with a class that is used to be handled in this way by male colleagues.

Behaviour that gives unintended sexual messages

Adult interactions with young people can be fraught with misunder-standings. Heads and teachers can unintentionally make some young people's lives a complete misery. For example, many young men, because of the way terms such as 'poof' and 'queer' are used in the playground, do not want to be labelled homosexual. At the time of writing, the Harvey Milk High School specifically for gay, lesbian, bisexual and transgender pupils is being established in New York 'because of the alarming rise in cases of harassment and assault . . . in the city's state schools' (Goffe, 2003, p. 10). It is often not pleasant to be deemed gay or lesbian in school. Consequently, many students avoid interactions with peers or adults that may encourage such assumptions.

Year 7 boys interviewed by Duncan (1999) had a 'surprising collective view of how they might detect gay activity' (p. 110). They described a [fantasy] scene where an 'innocent' boy is seduced by a homosexual teacher abusing his authority in a clandestine way. The teacher chooses a hard-working, well-behaved boy, not one of the more 'masculine' examples amongst which they included themselves, and asks him to remain behind after class.

> This is not a situation teachers would usually imagine could put their sexual reputation at risk. Such interactions with pupils take place many times in schools each day, but for these pupils it would signal some impropriety on the part of the teacher, and a dangerous situation for the boy.
>
> (Duncan, 1999, p. 110)

Sadly, in this school, as Duncan alludes, male teachers being friendly without any hidden agendas towards male pupils was not perceived as a possible way to behave:

> To be friendly with a boy, a teacher would have to play to the group, exert his masculine power and 'have a laugh'.
>
> (Duncan, 1999, p. 111)

The issue for school leaders is how can they change this sort of destructive culture when it is embedded in an institution particularly if it is accepted by most of the (male) stakeholders?

Targeted behaviour

With regard to more explicit behaviour, many would argue that teachers are in *loco parentis* of their pupils and consequently that sexual relationships between teachers and pupils are, whatever the circumstances, immoral. In some countries these issues are taken extremely seriously. Under Chinese law for example, any sexual assault on a person under the age of 14 is regarded as rape. In 2003, Li Feng, a 26-year-old teacher was executed for raping and molesting 19 girls under 14. The parents of 13 of these students then decided to sue the school for negligence asking for approximately £10,000 each (*TES*, 2003, p. 10).

The problem of sexual abuse between teachers and pupil is of particular concern in some parts of Africa including South Africa; Botswana (Woods, 2000); Malawi (Chitosi, 2000); and Zambia.

> Up to one in five girls are sexually abused at school by their teachers, the head of a leading aid agency said ahead of World

Aids day this Sunday . . . The ministry of education estimates that more than 1,000 teachers a year die of Aids . . . A popular myth that Aids can be cured by having sex with a virgin is adding to the problem.

(Splevins, 2002, p. 16)

The South African Council of Educators' Code of Conduct for teachers, published in 1999 specifically states that an educator must not 'harass learners, sexually or physically' (chapter 10, para. 1) and the South African minister of Education, Professor Kader Asmal has acknowledged the importance of the issue:

There must be an end to the practice of male teachers demanding sex with schoolgirls or female teachers. It shows selfish disrespect for the rights and dignity of women and young girls. Having sex with learners betrays the trust of the community. It is also against the law. It is a disciplinary offence. Tragically, nowadays, it is spreading HIV/AIDS and bringing misery and grief to these precious young people and their families.

(Asmal, 2000)

In Great Britain and Northern Ireland, as discussed in more detail by Graham Clayton in chapter 4, a consequence of the Sexual Offences (Amendment) Act 2000 (and re-enacted by the Sexual Offences Act, 2003) is that a teacher accused of sexual relations with a pupil could now face a criminal charge. This is regardless of whether the pupil is over the age of consent and/or the relationship is consensual. A conviction could result in imprisonment of up to five years.

It could be argued that there is a difference between a 'responsible' adult sexually abusing a young child and a young teacher embarking on a consensual relationship with a 17/18-year-old student. The former chief inspector of schools in England, Chris Woodhead is adamant that his well publicised relationship with an ex-pupil when he was a young (married) teacher did not start until she had left school. Nevertheless they first got to know each other in the context of teacher and pupil.[1]

In the past, relationships between young teachers and older students were not that uncommon and many resulted in marriage. One anonymous writer to the letters page of the TES said:

I'm writing in response to the story about the teacher sacked from his post in Newcastle for allegedly liaising with a female sixth-former. Attitudes have changed over the past 40 years towards this kind of relationship, as I myself was a sixth-former who went out with a young teacher at the school I attended. We met at the school's dance and the friendship grew, until we actually became engaged while I was still at school! The response was not to immediately sack the teacher, but rather the kindly old headmaster gave my husband-to-be advice on future financial management . . . We are about to celebrate our Ruby wedding anniversary . . . There is a fine distinction to be made between the dangers of teachers exploiting young pupils and a genuine relationship between an 18-year-old pupil and a 26-year-old teacher.

(*TES*, 30 January 2004, p. 25)

The case the letter writer cited concerned a 35-year-old teacher who claimed he was unfairly dismissed from a private church school for having a relationship with a sixth former. In spite of the fact that the tribunal panel believed that 'the respondent may have had a genuine belief in the applicant's guilt' the panel believed the teacher who claimed that the relationship had started after the young woman had left school. She moved in with him shortly before starting university. He won his case for unfair dismissal in February 2004 (BBC News website 28 February 2004).

In early 2004, BBC's Radio 4 broadcast a programme called *Married to Teacher*. Several men and women were interviewed about relationships they were involved in with their teachers whilst they were their pupils. One of the participants regretted the relationship and felt she had been exploited but the others (male and female) were still in touch with the teacher with whom they had experienced a sexual relationship. One couple had married and 24 years later were still together (Petty, 2004). Nevertheless an article in *The Times* related to the programme suggested:

The pupils in the documentary say their relationships with their teacher lovers were consensual. Yet a worrying sub-text runs through their accounts, with teenage pupils being drawn into an adult world of power games, deceit and complex emotions.

(Petty, 2004, pp. 6–7)

Yet it can be difficult for young teachers to deal with these situations. A 29-year-old teacher interviewed in the First Appointments section of the *TES* on this topic said:

> You don't get any training for that sort of problem and I think perhaps we should. . . . It is important to distinguish between a relationship which is abusive and one which is based on love. I don't think you can treat them the same.
>
> (Hook, 1999, p. 13)

Nevertheless, times and attitudes have changed. For example, as discussed above, some years ago it might have been considered acceptable for a young male teacher to have a relationship with a sixth former. Now it is seen as more problematic and a potential abuse of power. A spokesperson from the National Association of Schoolmasters and Union of Women Teachers, one of the major teachers' unions, said that the union would not condone such relationships:

> But it is a disciplinary matter and we don't see why teachers should be criminalized in this way.
>
> (Hook, 1999, p. 13)

In reality, the fact that sexual relations between teachers and pupils is now a criminal offence may make it more rather than less difficult for headteachers to deal with. Raising the stakes in this way increases the dilemma they face. Although they may abhor any suggestion of teachers being sexually involved with pupils, they may be unwilling to put events in motion that could result in a teacher ending up in jail. (See chapter 4 for more discussion on this.) Nevertheless:

> Recent cases [in the US] have sent a clear message to school officials that it is risky to ignore complaints of sexual misconduct involving school employees and students.
>
> (Curcio *et al.*, 1996, p. 38)

Indeed in Seattle, Washington State, in 2002, a young man called Vili F . . . and his mother sought damages of $1.9 million from the school district and the local police department for negligence of care. The suit involved a 34-year-old, married teacher, Mary Kay, who had a relationship with her 12-year-old pupil and became pregnant by him (the boy was then 13). Her husband told a relative who informed the Child Protective Services. In 1997 she pleaded guilty to second-degree rape of a child and after serving a six-month jail sentence, was released on probation. One of the conditions of her probation was that she was not to see the boy, but when she got pregnant by him a second time, her probation was revoked and she was sentenced to a seven-year term for child rape. According to the *Seattle Times* (Fryer, 2000) the boy, his mother (who looked after the two children) and the teacher co-wrote a book about the relationship, depicting it as a mutual love affair. However, the boy subsequently 'filed claims against the city of Des Moines and the Highline School District contending that public officials did not protect him from the sexual advances of a woman nearly three times his age' (p. 1). The jury rejected the claims of negligence and the case fell, but it took two years to resolve and at, no doubt, considerable financial cost to the public purse and personal cost to all those who had to testify.

Reported cases of women teachers becoming sexually involved with their pupils are still rare but do happen, as this case, the two reported in Chapter 1 and one of the participants in 'Married to teacher' demonstrate. Other examples have appeared in the US press in the recent past including that of Susan L a 38-year-old teacher from Mukilteo who was sentenced to five years in jail for having sex with one of her son's 14-year-old friends in 2002 and Jodi T, a 35-year-old seventh-grade teacher from New Jersey who was charged in 2003 for having sex with one of her 13-year-old students. (At the time of writing, this case is awaiting trial.)

As one commentator pointed out about the case of the Canadian supply teacher working in Surrey schools charged with five counts of indecent assault against three of her male pupils: '[the case] was more amusing than troubling . . . but would we have felt the same if the pupils were girls?' (Freely, 2002, p. 4). A 15-year-old boy being involved with a female teacher is seen as amusing, 'a school boy fantasy come true' and even a rite of passage. Reaction is different if the teacher is male when the pupil (male *or* female) is usually perceived to have been abused.

School leaders need to be mindful of double standards when dealing with these situations. Often though, they decide not to deal with the issues at all. A report commissioned by the Ontario government in Canada in 2000 indicated that children being sexually abused by teachers were frequently ignored by the authorities (Greenfield, 2001).

False allegations

School leaders who do confront these issues may find themselves dealing with a complex, drawn out and very difficult situation. (See chapter 6 for a first hand account.) It is such a complex area for school leaders, as unsubstantiated or ill-informed allegations can significantly affect and sometimes ruin teachers' lives.

Gay and lesbian teachers may be particularly vulnerable here. The type of bigotry demonstrated by the parent in the case of Neil, described in chapter 2, is often based on the assumption that gay and lesbian teachers will automatically have an inappropriate interest in their male/female pupils.

According to Barnard there were:

> A series of well-publicised cases where teachers were wrongly accused by pupils [of sexual abuse] and endured months of anxiety before being cleared . . . Last year, 114 school workers were convicted, cautioned, sacked or resigned under suspicion following allegations . . . But union figures suggest hundreds of allegations are made each year, with only a tiny minority reaching court.
>
> (*TES*, 16 June 2000, p. 9)

Subsequent to this news report, a poll was conducted by the National Association of Schoolmasters and Union of Women Teachers which revealed that 'allegations had been made against 1,742 teachers in the past decade but just 69 have been convicted' (Farrell, 2003a, p. 1). More recent figures show that 'the number is growing. 183 allegations were made in 2003 compared with 44 in 1991' (Williams, 2004, p. 11). The United Campaign Against False Allegations of Abuse, an umbrella organisation dealing with these issues held its inaugural meeting in London in September 2003. The organisation is campaigning to change the way investigations are carried out. According to Gayle Saunders, from Falsely Accused Carers and Teachers (Fact): 'Our biggest concern is with trawling – where police actively seek people to make accusations, often with the promise of compensation' (Farrell, 2003b, p. 15). A study by the Teacher Support Line, reported in the *TES* in December 2003, reported that calls to a teacher helpline revealed:

> A new trend of teachers suffering stress because they are the subject of malicious allegations is also emerging, the report

suggests. The helpline received more than 100 calls on this issue, even though it was not previously listed as a concern. Patrick Nash, TSL, chief executive, said: 'Teachers are frustrated by the lack of anonymity afforded to them and feel "guilty until proven innocent". Such allegations have a devastating effect on a teacher's life, family and career.' The figures were released as the National Association of Schoolmasters Union of Women Teachers was preparing to step up its campaign for anonymity for teachers facing malicious allegations. It says that fewer than 3 per cent of allegations of sexual, physical and verbal abuse made against teachers result in convictions.

(Lepkowska, Smith and Stewart, 2003, p. 3)

This concern needs to be addressed alongside the issues arising from the conviction in 2003 of the school caretaker, Ian Huntley for the murder of two girls in Soham. During the trial it was revealed that Huntley had previously been accused, but not convicted, of assaulting other girls and women. The information was not passed on to his new employer. This negligence was much criticised in the press at the time of the trial and in hindsight it is a stark omission. However, there remains an issue about people who are the subject of malicious allegations. If all allegations of a sexual nature are always to be passed on to employers, it is likely that many innocent people will find it exceedingly difficult, if not impossible, to obtain employment in jobs in education – teaching and support. For some, such as the potential teacher cited next there are alternatives – 'The NUT claims that one member who could not get a job in teaching because of disclosures of false allegations of abuse made against him finally joined the Metropolitan Police' (Williams, 2004, p. 13). However, for many, careers and indeed lives are ruined.

Some commentators suggest that we are in the midst of a moral panic about children and their vulnerability in the world outside their home (e.g. Wallace, 1997; Scott, 2001). In fact, in spite of the appalling but rare cases such as Soham, children are at greater risk in their own homes than outside them: 'three quarters of the perpetrators [of violent crime towards children] are parents and other relatives' (Wallace, 1997, p. 18). Nevertheless, the public perception and concern about the welfare of children has contributed to a climate where parents are worried and many teachers feel unable to physically comfort children for fear of being accused of sexual abuse.

because sex marks the boundary between childhood and adulthood, it is seen as the greatest threat to childhood. As a result, adults are increasingly seen as dangerous to children almost by definition – hence the inevitable demands for the protective government of children in environments where they interact with adults. This interaction is most easily regulated in public places such as schools, where children and adults must come into daily contact.

(Jones, 2001, p. 10)

Paradoxically, although there is more opportunity for sexual and physical abuse to occur in residential schooling, within a context of increasing concern about these issues, a growing number of parents in the UK are now sending their children to boarding schools. It is suggested that this phenomenon is at least partly due to the popularity of the Harry Potter books (Coward, 2001).

Maintaining a school climate where unwarranted and unwanted physical behaviour is outlawed, but appropriate physical behaviour is encouraged, is an enormous challenge for school leaders. (See Chapter 6 about guidelines on these issues.)

Pupils to teachers

As suggested earlier, sexual behaviour permeates the way many human beings relate to each other. In schools, particularly in secondary institutions, where young men and women are learning how to become adults, the exchange between adults and pupils is not only or always one way. This is particularly likely to be an issue among older pupils and the younger teachers. Curcio *et al.* suggest that most 'victims' are female teachers, but male teachers can also be tormented.

Wolpe (1988) notes:

how some girls behaved in the presence of some male teachers: they simpered, smiled and behaved in a generally coquettish fashion . . . They used body language and expressions that can be described as coquettish with the young 'dishy' male teachers . . . Those girls who practised this were participating in learning the scripts relating to adult sexual behaviour, and, at the same time, providing the others with a role model.

(pp. 119–32)

Other researchers have noticed similar behaviour. For example Epstein and Johnson (1998) observed: 'Tracy . . . was a young woman who was overt in her sexuality and constantly used it to bait the teachers' (p. 118).

Odone (2002) describing her own school days, wrote:

> many [girls] chose a teacher as the means of testing their power. And God help that teacher: he or she would be toyed with unscrupulously. Blackmailed, badmouthed, and bullied by their young tormentor . . . In the absence of boys, every girl at my all-girl school practised her teenage wiles on our male teachers. We had competitions to see who could make the science teacher blush . . . [We were] simply stepping into a long tradition of adolescents who try out their newfound sexual power on the most powerful adults in their lives.
>
> (p. 29)

Wolpe suggested that the girls she was researching did not behave like this with all teachers, not even with all male teachers. Their behaviour was targeted specifically at the young 'dishy' male teachers. By identifying teachers as sexually attractive, the girls were potentially both exerting power and making these teachers vulnerable.

One participant in the BBC radio programme *Married to Teacher* admitted that she as a 14-year-old had developed a crush on one of her teachers and had chased him until he had agreed to have a relationship with her (Petty, 2004).

Not all pupils making advances towards their teachers will do so in an aggressive manner. Wolpe observed that the sexual connotations of the boys' behaviour were often more subtle than that of the girls:

> The boys might act as protectors of some of the women teachers or simply set out to please them. This adds a further dimension to the rather one-sided view of boys as aggressive and sexually oppressive actors within the classroom situation.
>
> (Wolpe, 1988, p. 129)

Protectors are usually seen as more powerful than those who need protecting. If boys act as protectors towards their female teachers, this can make the teachers potentially vulnerable.

Some overtures will be callous and malicious; others will involve genuine feelings and perhaps consequently be even harder to deal with. In Khayyat (1992) quoted in Epstein and Johnson (1998, p. 147), a lesbian teacher talks about a pupil making advances to her:

> One of my students that summer, a young woman of about 19, took it upon herself to 'expose' my sexual preference. I knew that her intentions were not malicious but that she was acting out her attraction to me . . . The more she goaded me about my sexuality, the more I ignored her and the more she made her accusations publicly. Because my other students liked and respected me, their response was to silence her, to disbelieve and discredit her intimations that I was a lesbian. To them, I was a teacher they liked; therefore I could not be a lesbian.
>
> (pp. 1–2)

Boys learn from observing how to interact with their peers and adults. Older male pupils know that the power situation is not straightforward when they are interacting with their female teachers. Some of them have particular views about the place and role of women in society. Boys acting in a 'protective' way, as described by Wolpe, toward their female teachers will not always be doing so for 'gallant' reasons. Duncan (1999, p. 82) described the behaviour of one of the more challenging pupils in one of the schools he was researching:

> He displayed a calculating hardness in his interactions with both staff and pupils and was particularly stylish in his unnerving public chivalry: he could hold open a door for a teacher with a flourish that was at once courteous and threatening.

Wolpe described a woman teacher's interaction with older, 'deviant' boys in the following way:

> In passing she casually referred to their sexual behaviour. She said 'these boys made you aware of what you looked like . . . They used to make comments you know'. She did not find their comments offensive, on the contrary, she reacted in a traditionally feminine manner, accepting their comments as complimentary and gratifying. The boys were expressing their

approval of her as a woman, not a teacher. And this she did not find offensive . . . Their behaviour was quite at odds with their aggressive masculine sexuality which appears to be their trademark.

(1988, p. 127)

Beginning teachers and supply teachers are particularly vulnerable to displays of intimidating behaviour of a sexual nature from adolescent pupils. For example, in an English secondary school a girl was suspended for three days for 'sexually harassing' a trainee teacher. 'The 14-year-old was sent home from X school after she allegedly ripped open her blouse in front of XX, a technology teacher' (Lucas, 2004, p. 9).

Writing about the US context, Curcio *et al.* (1996) suggest that:

Sexual harassment of teachers ranges from physical intimidation . . . to suggestions from male students that they would be happy to 'service' female teachers. Teachers have endured obscene phone calls, comments about their bodies and sex lives, and obscene gestures.

(p. 37)

Teachers are also vulnerable to sexually intimidating behaviour from ex-pupils and from youths hanging around the school gate over whom they have no authority.

Both male and female teachers were subject to the power of non-pupils . . . [which] was significantly gendered. Male staff were much more likely to be threatened with physical aggression . . . with their *de facto* authority called into question. Female staff were more likely to be ignored or dismissed . . . as a spent force. Disempowered by their lack of *de jure* authority in their attempts to control behaviour outside of their remit, female staff were disrespected, often in a sexualised mode.

(Duncan, 1999, p. 90)

Sexual behaviour is complex. It exists in schools even though it may be unnoticed or ignored. By not confronting and addressing these issues educators are culpable of condoning behaviours that are not considered acceptable elsewhere in society. There is always though, the possibility that the consequence of confrontation will be a reactionary backlash. Nevertheless, headteachers will need to understand the issues in order to find ways of addressing them. The following chapter explores these issues.

Note

1   This is not to condone such relationships. However slight the age gap and regardless of who is the initiator, whilst in a teacher/pupil relationship there is an important power relationship and professional responsibility not to be involved in such liaisons. My point is to indicate that the scale of the transgression is different.

Part II

Some solutions

Chapter 4

Brief encounters

Dealing with the law

Graham Clayton

Introduction

This chapter is not a comprehensive description of the law describing the legal consequences for teachers behaving badly. Nor is it a detailed guide on avoiding the pitfalls of the law. The purpose of the chapter is rather to explore why there is law to deal with sexual relationships involving children and young people, directly and indirectly. What are the beliefs in our society which give rise to law and what objectives does the law serve? What does the law require of teachers both in terms of the protection they must give to children and in the example they are required to set?

I hope this analysis will aid understanding and increase self-confidence in dealing with the law and its agencies of enforcement. Law is, by definition, threatening. Its institutions are intimidating. In every courtroom we are confronted by the symbols of the authority of the state and the crown.

We prefer to think that, as law abiding subjects of the crown, we are obedient to the law because we respect it and believe in it, but there are few of us who have not, at some time, exceeded speed limits and slowed down when we see a police car sitting waiting to catch the miscreant motorist. We do that of course not because we respect our obligations to maintain steady conformity with the limits imposed by law but because we fear the consequences of being caught in our failure to comply.

Law prohibits the expression of our more selfish desires. We may wish to arrive more quickly at our destinations or perhaps we just like speed, but the law says that we must restrain ourselves because our speed will unacceptably threaten others. We may wish to be wealthy, to have possessions and selfishly enjoy them, but the law insists that we may only acquire them lawfully. Looked at in this way, law becomes less a question of personal morality and rather more a matter of pragmatic self-restraint under threat of penalty, that threat being greater by degree depending on the level of social disapproval. When the law is concerned with matters of sexual morality and conduct, fear of legal consequences is heavily overlaid with fear of condemnation from moral opinion. So, this chapter aims to offer some distinctions between strictly legal requirements and moral imperatives, to assist school leaders in their exercise of professional judgement.

The above analysis of the law, of course, is a very cynical one, better reserved for sociologists and criminologists. Its significance here is to illustrate only that cynical analysis is possible, and from that to construct for school leaders a rational basis for self-confidence in professional judgement. The modern approach to law, as evidenced by the Sexual Offences Act 2003 and the repeal of the infamous Section 28, has significantly shifted in favour of the perhaps more cynical, or better, the more pragmatic and realistic approach: that it is not the role of the state through mechanisms of punitive law to dictate moral conduct. Rather, the role of the state, through law, is to protect the vulnerable from harm and to protect the social cohesiveness and positive progressive development of the state itself. With this sort of understanding, school leaders who have responsibility for developing young minds and protecting youngsters from that exploitation of their vulnerability which impedes their educational development, may gain justified confidence in the collective judgement of the profession to which they belong.

In an effort to achieve this objective, the chapter starts with an explanation of the sexual offences law. It then progresses to deal with the legal issues for teachers as role models in those standards of conduct which continue to be regarded as healthy and positive in a mature, well balanced and broadly tolerant society, which values diversity and stands against irrational prejudice. It is a step by step approach. It examines the newly devised certainties of the criminal law in the form of the Sexual Offences Act. It then considers the more subjectively determined penalties for bad behaviour permitted by employment law. It then concludes with some thoughts about the future prospect of a self-governed teaching profession on collectively determined standards of conduct. It is likely that, in the end, these standards will prove to be the standards of liberalism and tolerance which have guided teachers as educators through several generations, standards now to be refreshed and applied to the twenty-first century.

In the last quarter of a century the concepts of liberal education, provided by a mature profession governed by its own traditions of excellence, have been dominated, diffused, perhaps even confused, by policy imperatives favouring high levels of accountability. If this chapter and this book help teachers to secure an influence on the development of the law leaving only teachers who really behave badly to fear it, a step forward will have been taken towards the recreation of a self-confident profession trusting in itself and being prepared to assert openly its modest self-assurance.

Passion in parliament

It is a fondly held belief that the law occupies a place far distant from the centres of debate, opinion, dogma and bigotry; that it has, in some way, an objective equality which makes it essentially fair so that all may be equal under it. This is a belief worth preserving and respecting, because it is something which forces law makers and judges at least to try to preserve objectivity and fairness within the law. Without it, we would be accepting the legitimacy of majority control of the punitive process of law with all the dangers of oppression of minorities and the dictatorship of bigotry.

It is, however, unavoidable that the law is in some part, a reflection of the times in which it is made, with much of the judgemental prejudice that prevails in public opinion at that time. The law, after all, is made by people with opinions. Now that so much of it is made in parliament as the outcome of debate, the opinions of judges derived from their social background are far less influential in the making of law than even fifty years ago. However, greater democracy in the law-making process has not necessarily brought greater objectivity. On the contrary, the dominance of what communicators have called the ruling class in the law-making process has been replaced by the dominance of what government ministers and members of parliament judge to be the public opinion from which they take their mandate. Moreover, since politicians are by definition opinionated people, it is not necessarily the case that their contribution to law-making is representative of public opinion, as opposed to their own.

One cannot be cynically critical of this. Law which is made by humans by any process has inevitable defects and deficiencies, but it is important to recognise the inevitability of imperfection in order to explain the law and to temper its application with practical common sense.

That, however, has proved to be no simple task when the subject matters are (1) children and (2) sex. Few people are without opinion on either. Put the two subjects together with the aim of making some law and highly volatile and outraged opinion is sure to be encountered.

No one need look far to find the proof of this. Take what has been known as Section 28, the prohibition of the promotion by local authorities of the teaching of the acceptability of homosexuality as a pretended family relationship. As law, it was horribly drafted and, as a result, virtually meaningless. It never came to be enforced by a court but it generated a huge volume of heated debate and was very difficult to get rid of, finally dying a prolonged and almost Shakespearean demise. (See chapter 1 for more discussion on Section 28.)

The same was true of the Sexual Offences Act of 1956. By 2002, this statute was in a tattered and sorry state, but it had to get so bad that the law makers in parliament would have no choice but to replace it, before the promoters of change would dare to embark on the debate. Even then, the Sexual Offences Bill, introduced in January 2003, appeared first in the House of Lords where it could be considered in a rather more sedate and less publicly scrutinised environment. Despite that, it still became the subject of high controversy.

If all that were not enough, the summer of 2003 also saw parliamentary passions inflamed over the UK implementation of a European Union equality directive banning job discrimination on grounds of 'sexual orientation'. Rather than implement the directive as written in Brussels, the UK government chose to rewrite the UK legislation in its own terms and immediately ran into a row with teachers about the exceptions to the standard protection, which would, it was said, allow discrimination against gay teachers working in church schools.

The unfortunate outcome is that the resulting law is at risk of being a rather messy compromise, enabling all those who participated in the highly charged debate from which the law was made, to claim it victoriously as their own. There is no commonly acknowledged understanding of what the law is and those such as teachers, who have a responsibility to apply and work with the law in some of its most sensitive areas, are left without the confidence to answer others who accuse them of failure to comply. In these circumstances, caution and fear tend to give practical authority to the more illiberal interpretations.

Sex and sensitivity

Telling teachers that sex and sexuality are highly sensitive subjects in schools, is likely to produce the scornful enquiry as to whether the well meaning adviser has read a newspaper in the last fifty years. Explaining that the law is, in some respects, as volatile and uncertain as the public opinion from which the law derives, is more disconcerting. Teachers prefer to feel that, whilst they know themselves to be vulnerable to public opinion, they can at least depend on the mature rationality of law to protect them.

To some extent teachers can rely on law in this way, but here the aim is also to encourage teachers in their own self-confidence to deal with issues of sex and sexuality, asserting that where the law does represent inadequate compromise, its practical application is best left in the hands of mature and skilled professionals, who understand the circumstances for which the law is made. This is never to say that laws can be ignored by a teacher who believes it to be wrong in a given situation. That would be an unacceptable presumption. There is, however, good reason to trust in the principle that good law serves good purpose and should not be used as an instrument of prejudice and bigotry.

The criminal law

The Sexual Offences Act 2003 replaces a mid-twentieth-century enactment which was very largely concerned only with the predatory and exploitative sexual conduct of males. In the 1956 Sexual Offences Act, there was a clear element of moral distaste by the predominantly male legislators of that time for what they considered to be sexual perversions and excesses of their own gender. Their preparedness to criminalise perceived male immorality was accompanied by the patronising assumption that female immorality was the consequence of male exploitation and of itself did not warrant criminalisation.

The Sexual Offences Act 2003 has a much more rationally satisfactory foundation. It tends strongly towards the increasingly accepted theoretical basis for criminal law, that the state has no business criminalising private morality which does no harm to others without their consent. Even if dominant public morality disapproves of conduct outside the mainstream, it is not for the state to use the machinery of the criminal law to force conformity to mainstream morality. The role of the criminal law is, rather, to punish and deter conduct against which citizens should be protected by the state.

Apart from those offences which, by definition, can only be committed by a man, the 2003 Act is also gender neutral, making no assumptions that women can be any less guilty than men of the various offences for which the Act provides.

Consistent with the overall approach of criminalising the conduct of those who do harm and so protect the unwilling victims of harm, the Act is particularly concerned with the protection of children. Children are not regarded as competent to give consent to conduct which would otherwise be criminal. Sexual penetration and other sexual contact will amount to rape or sexual assault if committed on a child under 13 regardless of whether the child has consented. Harsher maximum sentences may be applied if these offences are committed against under 13s.

The Act also creates offences of which children may unequally be victims:

- sexual activity with a child;
- causing a child to engage in sexual activity;
- inciting a child to engage in sexual activity;
- engaging in sexual activity in the presence of a child;
- causing a child to watch a sexual act;
- arranging or facilitating a child sex offence;
- meeting a child following sexual grooming.

In relation to most of these offences the Act makes a distinction between children under 13 and those under 16. A person accused of such an offence against a child aged 13, 14 or 15 has a defence if he or she can show a reasonable belief that the child was 16 or over when the incident took place. Otherwise the Act provides for different maximum sentences depending on the age of the guilty party and the extent of the sexual activity involved.

Special provision is then made to deal with child sex abuse within families. Young persons up to age 18 are protected by the criminal law from adult chasers in close family relationships. People of any age with mental disorders and learning disabilities are also specially protected.

It is an exceptionally serious offence to obtain the services of a child prostitute, to cause or incite a child to be a prostitute or to be involved in pornography or to control child prostitution.

The 2003 Act also re-enacts the provisions of the Sexual Offences (Amendment) Act 2000 which established the series of sexual offences occurring by the abuse of a position of trust held by a person aged 18 or over in relation to a person under 18. These offences may be committed against children up to age 16 coincident with the general range of child sex offences, but exceptionally they may also be committed against young persons aged 16 and 17. The accused has a defence if he or she can demonstrate a reasonable belief that a child was 18 or over (provided the child was at least 13) or if he or she can demonstrate a reasonable belief that there was not in fact a position of trust (provided again that the child was at least 13). The offences are sexual touching, causing or inciting the child or young person to engage in sexual activity, engaging in sexual activity in the presence of the child or young person and causing the child or young person to watch a sexual act.

Teachers are specifically identified as being in a position of trust in relation to any child or young person in full-time education if the teacher has a regular involvement in caring for, training or supervising the child. None of these offences are committed if the teacher is lawfully married to the 'child' nor can conduct which predates the position of trust be an offence under these provisions.

The Protection of Children Act 1978 (which is further amended by the Sexual Offences Act 2003) governs the offence of making indecent photographs of children. This includes the downloading of child pornography onto computers.

All these offences are punishable not only by fines and, in most cases, imprisonment but also by registration on the register of sex offenders formerly maintained under the Sexual Offenders Act 1997 and now under Part 2 of the Sexual Offences Act 2003.

Causing offence

This is not of course a comprehensive study of the law on sex offences, even of those involving children. There is much more detail in the Sexual Offences Act itself, in the Children Act 1989 and elsewhere. Significant here is the examination of the impact of the criminal law in 'protecting' children, and the special status in the criminal law of those who are in a position of trust in relation to children and young persons.

Without doubt in the enactment of the Sexual Offences Act, parliament has, on the whole, reflected the mainstream moral judgement of a society more liberal and more reasoned than that of 1956. Though there has been some heated debate on particular issues about the potential of some of the language of the 2003 Act to strike at generally accepted behaviour, the overall approach is one which most people, particularly parents, will applaud. The strong emphasis given to child-related sex offences protects children, and the vast majority of parents will be rightly gratified that it is so.

The job having been done well to the reasonable satisfaction of practical observers and commentators, the philosophical analysis is of limited interest – not for the purpose of promoting a more libertarian reform but only to contain the law within the confines of its underlying principles, and to assist those who must apply and implement it, to do so with confidence.

That said, it is by no means as easy to find consistency in the underlying philosophy as it is to justify the law in the context of accepted sexual morality. The predatory male against whom the 1956 Act was directed has become the predatory adult in 2003. The criminal law assumes the vulnerability of the child to adult abuse and exploitation. In this sense, the law is essentially patronising. It continues to demand, under pain of criminal penalty, socially acceptable conduct towards a social group arbitrarily assumed, without exception, to be incapable of relevant fault, and therefore vulnerable to exploitation which the state must prevent.

As a parent, like other parents, as a lawyer and as someone working closely with teachers, I feel very strongly in favour of this law, because it protects children against pretty unpleasant people whose motives are self-gratifyingly evil against the backdrop of our accepted social order and sexual morality. Nonetheless it remains a feature of the law on sexual offences that it criminalises behaviour that victimises others because of their age rather than their humanity. No reader should mistake this observation as a criticism which offers an excuse for libertarianism in the law which protects children. It is, however, an observation which may assist the reader in better understanding of why the law is so difficult to construct and to have more confidence in applying the result.

It means that the law is as it is because, as a society, as a state, we have resolved that this is how it must be. And it is this which explains and defines the role of those who have responsibility in any form, for rearing children into adulthood. What the criminal law does is to declare certain forms of human behaviour to be such that paedophiles must be ostracised, deterred and punished at the initiative of the state. The line which defines that conduct as 'off-limits' is where the interference of the state's criminal justice system begins and ends. Where that line is to be drawn has been very much part of the long debate over the decriminalisation of soft drug usage.

But that does not mean that all forms of behaviour free of criminality are acceptable in other forms of relationship and interaction. On the contrary, accepted morality will still dictate standards in other forms of social and economic relationship, with the support of the civil rather than the criminal law. The civil law will permit the imposition of penalties by one person against another to enforce accepted moral standards. We can see this particularly in what the law permits or does not prohibit in employment relationships and in the relatively new statutory regime of professional standards enforced by the General Teaching Councils in England and Wales.

Abuse of trust

Close to this line between the state's deployment of the criminal justice system and the law governing employment statutes and employment relationships, is the criminalisation of abuse of trust, controversially first enacted in 2000.

There is no serious dispute that there is an issue here over conduct which is to be condemned. However, the descriptive language is in itself odd and it is there that the difficulties begin. The phrase 'position of trust' is inadequate in terms of everyday language since what is being addressed is a great deal more than simply being 'trusted'. In legal terms, the 'position of trust' is very different from that of a trustee in property law. The definition in context describes someone who has responsibility, normally by virtue of an employment, for the care, training or supervision of a legal 'minor'.

We see then that, in fact, we do not have a definition in which the actual existence of trust placed by the minor in the adult is the test. The adult is inescapably in the position of trust by virtue of his or her position, by virtue of what he or she *is* in relation to the minor, not by virtue of what their relationship actually is.

The criminal law impacts most significantly on relationships between over 18s and 16 and 17-year-olds. Abuse of trust offences against under 16s are offences in any event. An abuse of trust offence in these cases is an additional concurrent offence. We must bear in mind too that the offence is not committed against a minor to whom the adult is lawfully married. So, what we have is a situation in which a 22-year-old teacher who engages in heavy petting with a 17-year-old student of his or hers is guilty of a criminal offence, but only if committed outside a lawful marriage.

This example was used to question whether 'abuse of trust' should ever be the subject of a distinct criminal offence at all. Other examples prevailed. It is obviously a great deal easier for some commentators to find justification in strong condemnation of the predatory male menopausal teacher who callously exploits the crush of an impressionable 16-year-old female student, or the voracious middle-aged female lecturer who wantonly works her way through a class full of student 'toy boys'. But, even if these stereotypes really exist, they provide very curious models on which to fashion criminal law.

Nonetheless, we must again accept that there is a prevailing sentiment which senses an evil to be addressed. The message we are getting is that something special is being expected of some people who are in a particular position in the system as a whole.

Section 28: infamy, infamy, they've all got it in for me

The most extreme example, the loudest message, comes from the infamous 'Section 28', which never was, in fact, Section 28 at all, but Section 2A of the Local Government Act 1986, inserted by Section 28 of the Local Government Act 1988.

Section 2A was not within the boundaries of the criminal law. Indeed, it is not entirely clear what it was and, since it was never relied upon in any proceedings before a court, we never had the benefit of authoritative judicial explanation. It created no crime and it was far from clear how it governed relationships between people. Having been cobbled together in an effort to satisfy sufficient support to secure a majority in parliament, its language was, to say the least, inelegant. Despite this, even the hint of a suggestion that it ought to be repealed provoked, for many years, purple outrage amongst anti-libertarians whose certainty of opinion gave the impression that they could not actually have read it.

Section 2A actually provided:

> A local authority shall not:
> a) intentionally promote homosexuality or publish material with the intention of promoting homosexuality; and
> b) promote the teaching in any maintained school of the acceptability of homosexuality as a pretended family relationship.

It was, in fact, only ever a prohibition against a particular use of public money by local authorities. The presumed remedy would then lie in a legal action by outraged council tax payers against councillors. So far as schools were concerned, the Education Reform Act, passed in the same year that Section 2A was enacted, began the process of transferring management of schools to governing bodies. Before long, it became impossible to see how a local authority could ever promote anything in most schools if the governors did not want it.

As if this were not enough to render Section 2A legally ineffective, its language completed the job. Homosexuality is a stage of being, not a relationship, and as some more mischievous lawyers pointed out, even if sense could be made of the English grammar, the sentence did not actually prohibit the promotion of the teaching of homosexuality as a real (as opposed to 'pretended') family relationship. Since those who make out the case for same-sex parenting want full acceptance and have nothing to do with pretence, then on this interpretation, Section 2A gave them precisely what they sought.

However, as the prolonged argument over its repeal proved, Section 2A was very effective indeed outside the courts. It provided the focus for the debate on how teachers should relate to their pupils in matters to do with sex and, in turn, their role model identity. Whilst Section 2A existed with the interpretations its protagonists sought to give it, it served to reinforce, all the doubts and fears of teachers. Its repeal, in September 2003, leaves a vacuum to be filled by a new agenda.

No less significant than the repeal has been the failure of the attempts, led in the House of Lords by the formidable Baroness Blatch, to replace it. Her efforts, if successful, would have resulted in the enormously expensive and time-consuming requirement on school managers to supply copies of all sex education materials to parents. Lord Brightman also weighed in with a proposal to prohibit local authorities from promoting 'any particular sexual lifestyle', whilst specifically reaffirming support for 'the institution of marriage'.

The rejection of these attempts at further statutory interference in teaching about sex is, these days, a very welcome but all too unusual expression of confidence in teachers to do what they do responsibly and professionally. It is a gesture of confidence on which to build.

Themes and trends

Let us then pause to take stock of what all this detail of law and political sensitivity means for teachers. What are the themes and trends we can perceive in the debates on the Sexual Offences Bill and related legislation? To summarise:

1   Law generally does not, in fact, have the intellectual certainty in which we like to trust when we accept obedience to the rule of law. It is the product of prevailing attitude. Particularly in areas in which law governs subjects of sensitivity in society, the law does not have philosophical parity, nor even necessarily philosophical consistency. It is not national law, but only the product of the society for which it is made. It is to be respected for that alone.

2   The criminal law penalises conduct which legislators determine to be beyond toleration by the state. The line by which the state's toleration is delineated may, in some cases, be arbitrarily drawn. The law on sexual offences provides a clear example.

3   The new law on sexual offences has a focus on the protection of children who are assumed to be vulnerable to exploitation and abuse. Their assumed vulnerability reduces according to age with lines drawn, again arbitrarily, at 13, 16 and 18.

4   At the third stage, 16 and 17-year-olds, their vulnerability is protected particularly from those who have special responsibilities, described as positions of trust, towards them.

5   Legislators may continue to try to control or influence the teaching and training of legal minors in sexual matters, through controls on public service provision of education in an uncertain area between the criminal law and the civil law governing relations between individuals.

We then see just how crucial is the role of teachers in the scheme of sex related law. Starting with our analysis of the criminal law, we have moved beyond its boundaries into other areas dealing with the development of the sexual morality of children growing to adulthood.

Teachers are special

From all this, we can tell that teachers are in a special position. The law has expectations peculiar to teachers. However, since the decline of 'in loco parentis' as a meaningful concept, we have no short encapsulation of what that position is.

Despite 'in loco parentis' the courts have never, in fact, considered teachers as having authority and responsibility delegated to them by parents. Cases such as *Spiers* v. *Warrington Corporation* (1953) illustrate that teachers have a freestanding authority in law to make and enforce rules regardless of the standards of discipline adopted by parents. Their legal responsibility for the protection of pupils against physical harm is in modern law a responsibility based on a duty of care owed by them as teachers rather than as parent substitutes. This is clearly reinforced by the abandonment of the notion that children are somehow in the ownership of their parents. The Children Act of 1989 clearly conferred an independent legal status on the child, a status which continues to be reinforced by the still developing concern of the state, at the initiative of government, for child protection and child welfare. In *Williamson* v, *Secretary of State for Education and Employment* (2003), the Court of Appeal has resisted the argument that the statutory ban on corporal punishment in independent schools infringes the human rights of parents who believe in 'mild' corporal punishment.

Broader debates and conflicts add to the uncertainty over teachers' role model status and their responsibilities. Concerns over teacher workload and stress touch on questions about when responsibility ends – at the school gate or when the bell rings. What of the proposed new workforce of higher level teaching assistants (HLTAs)? Will they take on the role model status and responsibilities of qualified teachers? The abuse of trust provisions of the Sexual Offences Act certainly seem to be sufficiently widely drawn to apply to HLTAs with teaching responsibilities, but to what extent will the burdens of teachers as moral guardians and role models now extend to them? What additional responsibility will qualified teachers have for the moral conduct and standards of HLTAs who assist and support them? It is not apparent that answers to these and many similar questions have been thought through as the proposal begins to be implemented in 2003.

We need, in this atmosphere of uncertainty, to try to get a better handle on where today's teachers really are in this moral maze.

Employment law and bad behaviour

Some assistance can be gained from employment rights law, though this too is clouded by the uncertainties of the unique relationship governing the employment of teachers. Employment generally in UK law has a contractual foundation. It is a relationship governed by agreement between employer and employee. In nineteenth- and early twentieth-century law, it was an openly agreed relationship, then described as one of master and servant, free of intervention by state authority. However, driven by employee demands for more strength in their contract bargaining position, from the early 1960s parliament began to intervene by creating a statutory platform of statutory employment rights from which there could be no contracting out. Fuelled then by the demands for economic convergence amongst the European Community members, the platform has been raised and enlarged so that the free bargaining of contractual terms takes place now, only in a much diminished space above the statutory platform.

For teachers, this space is exceptionally small, since pay, duties and working time are determined by a review body and given effect by Order in Parliament.

There is even widespread understanding about who the employers of teachers are. The law is actually clear on this point. The employer/employee contract for a teacher in community and voluntary controlled schools is between the teacher and the LEA. Teachers in voluntary aided and foundation schools have contracts with the particular school governing body.

The misunderstandings arise because, although they are not employers, the governing bodies of community and voluntary controlled schools have some important powers of an employer conferred on them by Acts of Parliament. Amongst these are the power to control staff discipline and the power to have a teacher removed from their school for disciplinary reasons. A decision to this effect by a governing body is almost certain to bring about the teacher's dismissal.

Governing bodies of voluntary aided and foundation schools have all the powers of employers to dismiss. Prior to 1988, when LEAs were in charge of dismissal decisions, in relation to teachers in what we now know as community and voluntary schools, there were only 104 LEAs making these decisions and there was a reasonably reliable consistency in their approach to teacher misconduct. Now we have 25,000 different decision-making bodies made up of people who reflect the full spectrum of opinion on what should be considered moral and sexual misconduct.

Voluntary aided schools are, of course, mostly what are increasingly now known as 'faith' schools and although there are special statutory safeguards for teachers who do not share the religious opinions of the followers of the organised church which supports the school, they are all employed subject to a standard contractual term that they will not conduct themselves in a way that is offensive to the faith. There has been a prolonged 'stand-off' between the Anglican and Catholic school authorities and the main teachers' organisations over this clause. The churches clearly have no intention of giving way, but they have deftly avoided bringing the clause into a highlight of controversy for over fifty years. Nonetheless, the potential exists for confrontation, for example, whenever a teacher working in a Catholic voluntary aided school remarries following a divorce. There may never be a major clash between teachers and the churches over this clause, but this very clear example demonstrates that there is no commonly understood definition of a badly behaving teacher.

Anti-discrimination laws have, since 1975, protected employees generally against discrimination in employment on ground of marital status as part of the regime which outlaws discrimination on grounds of gender. In 2003 these protections were extended, to give effect in the UK to a European Union directive, with the effect of outlawing discrimination on grounds of religious belief (or the absence of it) and discrimination on grounds of sexuality. However the directive permits these protections to be set aside in circumstances where an employer can justify discrimination which can reasonably be considered necessary for the purposes of an organised religion. The UK government has chosen to implement the EU directive in its own terms and, as soon as the UK regulations were made, they were challenged as an inadequate implementation of the EU directive by teachers' organisations, fearing that the teachers working or seeking to work in faith schools could be without the legal protection to which they should be entitled.

The law which gives protection against unfair dismissal is effective in preventing, or at least deterring, irrational prejudice and plain bigotry in defining teacher misconduct. However, it is a long-established principle of employment protection law that it is not the role of employment tribunals, through which the protection is enforced, to substitute their judgments for those of an employer. Employment tribunals are much more the guardians of fair procedures in employment discipline than they are arbiters of the substance of the case. It did look for a short while at the beginning of this decade that the employment tribunals might be more interventionist, but this trend was quickly reversed. It has been reaffirmed that an employment tribunal should not find that a claimant has been unfairly dismissed because the tribunal members would not have dismissed him if they had been making the employer's decision. If that decision falls within the broad band of reasonable responses of an employer to fairly ascertained conclusions of fact, it is no business of the employment tribunal to upset it.

So, again, though we can identify helpful themes from employment law as to how teacher misconduct ought to be investigated, we can gain nothing in terms of objective definition of what bad behaviour on the part of teachers really is.

Bad behaviour and the right to work

Outside the framework of the employment relationship we have mechanisms, also of long standing but recently expanded, by which teachers are called to account for misconduct. This was the process by which teachers ended up on List 99, now replaced by the much broader Register of Persons Considered Unsuitable to Work with Children. List 99 was often spoken of as some darkly concealed 'enemies' list, administered by the faceless figures of a secret police. It was actually nothing of the kind. It was a list of teachers whose teaching certificates had been withdrawn because of their convictions for criminal offences or other findings of serious misconduct. No name appeared on the list without his or her first having had the opportunity to make representations to Department for Education officials as to why it should not with the exception only of those who had disappeared and could not be traced. The 'secrecy', or rather the limited availability of the list, was to prevent its misuse.

The Register remains under the control of government departments. It is still the DfES which decides the professional fate of teachers found guilty of serious misconduct involving children, including those convicted of sexual offences. However, this now operates alongside the much wider regime of registration administered by the General Teaching Councils for England and for Wales established by and under the Teaching and Higher Education Act 1998.

General Teaching Councils (GTCs) – at last

In the following chapter, David James deals in detail with the role of the GTCs. I will not trespass on his territory except to set the role of the GTCs into the context of the legal framework.

The teachers' organisations eagerly sought the establishment of the General Teaching Councils; but their aspirations were much more aspirations of principle than detailed proposals. The model with which they were finally rewarded was not quite what they had in mind. When the GTCs proclaimed themselves the 'new voices for teachers' with talk of 'members' and 'subscriptions,' the representative teachers' organisations understandably took offence. Their protests were boosted by teacher support when it appeared that the government intended to finance the GTCs by compulsory deductions from teachers' pay packets.

The GTCs wisely retreated. 'Subscriptions' were more accurately acknowledged to be 'fees'. The concept of mass 'membership' was dropped and the GTCs altered their vocal status to that of voices for *teaching* with subtle changes in their public pronouncements to match. The GTCs were then able to settle down to carving out their identity much more in line with the model to which the teachers' organisations had aspired. It is a model which rightly includes concern for standards of conduct amongst members of the teaching profession.

GTC registration is legally compulsory for any teacher employed to work at a school. Without it, the teacher cannot teach in a maintained school. The requirement provides the means for the GTCs to exercise their professional regulations and disciplinary powers. They can withdraw, suspend or qualify registration as a penalty against teachers who behave badly. Their practice is not arbitrary. They have well thought through procedures fully conforming to the principles of fairness and natural justice.

There are very special features about the General Teaching Councils which make them so important in the future development of attitudes to teachers behaving badly.

Accentuate the positive

Readers may have noticed what has been discussed in this chapter is predominantly a process of negative identification of bad behaviour. The good thing about 'in *loco parentis*' was that it gave a positive identity to teacher role model status. It defined the status and standard of grace from which teachers might fall. The decline in meaning and validity of the in *loco parentis* principle has left a vacuum. The law has drifted into a negative identification of bad behaviour. Its strong emphasis is on deterrence, the enforcement of good conduct by the threat of penalty, whether in the criminal courts, by employment penalties or professional disqualification. The overall effect is very damaging. Deterrence creates the climate of fear, the insidious erosion of self-confidence. There is no longer a clearly acknowledged standard of professional conduct. Teachers moderate and dilute their professional judgements about the role models they offer out of fear of their accountability to authority which holds potentially draconian legal powers.

Until we have clarity in a clear code constructed out of the experience and understanding of the teaching profession itself, with legal force and with mechanisms for fair and objective judgement, teachers, and headteachers in particular, will continue to face uncertainty and will continue to feel threatened by often condemnatory and highly subjective opinions about what is and what is not proper in their relationships with children. There is no comprehensive list of 'dos and don't's', no certainty in danger signs for which to watch, no checklist of questions for interviews.

There cannot be. A question asked at interview which, when set against a background of good reasons for doubt and suspicion, may be a fair and searching question, can easily be the foundation for a perfectly proper complaint of unlawful discrimination from a teacher whose professionalism and integrity are in fact beyond question, but whose sexual orientation has been stereotypically and prejudicially considered to give credibility to suspicion. An ill founded allegation to which there is over-reaction on the part of managers can cause deep and prolonged distress to the accused, and be a cause for legal action by the accused for compensation.

And yet, an allegation lightly cast aside and assumed to be false, may, of course, be hugely distressing if later it turns out to have been true and further incidents occur. Those who have ignored the first allegation will feel all the guilt about what they could have prevented and there will be no shortage of critics ready to attribute blame.

There is however one guideline which does help in avoiding problems. It can be summed up in one word – talk. Professional misconduct on the part of a teacher is his or her guilty secret. Managers who create an environment in which it is possible to talk about the risk factors in non-threatening ways are much more likely to be able to spot real problems than those who allow doubts to remain unaddressed and suspicions to remain the subject of rumour. The headteacher who shows himself or herself willing to give positive and constructive counsel to the perhaps naive but innocent teacher is much more likely to be able to detect serious problems at an early stage than the one who makes every slightly inappropriate remark or contact an issue for haughty reprimand. If a young teacher appears just that bit too enthusiastic in one-to-one relationships with pupils, be prepared to give mature guidance without being threatening. If a teacher's lessons appear to be heavy on sexual innuendo and personal familiarities, talk it through constructively and professionally. Unless the matter is obviously serious in a way which makes some clear warning necessary, give the teacher concerned confidence that this is a talk about professional development, not the beginning of an embarrassing disciplinary process. Let the problem or potential problem be aired openly and maturely.

In most cases, this should cause any necessary adjustment in behaviour. Just very, very occasionally, something may be detected in the response or demeanour of the teacher which gives cause for concern. It may be something you would never have discovered if you had not shone the light on it. In the end the setting of standards with which this chapter is concerned should come from talking, from teachers sharing their professionalism with each and building a collective confidence in knowing what is right, what is wrong and what to be cautious about.

The demand for teacher accountability has gone quite out of control. There are still shrill voices insisting that teachers are insufficiently accountable, but the obvious truth is very different. Multiple agencies, authorities and pressure groups possess the authority of law to call upon teachers for the performance of legally defined obligations, governing bodies, local education authorities, OFSTED, the government, the examination boards, child protection authorities, the police, the General Teaching Councils, parent committees and a host of other quangos. Most of them have legal powers to impose penalties directly on teachers and the rest have legal rights to seek those penalties. Their demands are often conflicting. The exercise of their powers has no consistency.

Cast into this simmering cauldron of uncertainty the subject of sex and it boils. No one need look further than the Hansard records of the debates on the Sexual Offences Act and Section 28 to see the passion that is evoked.

Whether or not the government has been right to adopt the highly expensive and extremely complicated mechanism for funding the GTCs is an unfinished debate. It has certainly been right to emphasise the desirability of giving teachers a sense of ownership of the GTCs. The Councils are constituted as partnerships of teachers and representatives of other education stakeholders with teachers as the senior partners. The teacher groups on the councils are partly nominees of the representative teacher organisations and others directly elected. The teacher organisation nominees already have a wealth of experience in setting and adjudicating standards of professional conduct. The NUT has a long established Code of Professional Conduct built into its rules which it regularly implements to expel serious miscreants from membership.

As the GTCs settled into their more comfortable role of advocacy for *teaching* rather than undemocratically claiming to be representative of *teachers*, the Councils began the task of drawing up their own Code of Professional Standards. It is specifically declared not to be a set of rules, the breach of which will automatically expose teachers to legal penalty. It is instead a code based on the professional commitment of teachers themselves to those standards of conduct which they believe will contribute positively to the education of children. It benefits from the experience of that sense of professionalism which is well understood within the teacher organisations, and it benefits from the understanding of classroom practitioners to whom the GTCs can offer a new opportunity for self-confident expression. The code benefits too from constructive contributions of representatives of the many stakeholders in education.

Everything about Section 28 proved a point which, for lawyers, is fundamental. Mere declaratory statements giving expression to opinion are not law in a true sense. The law is essentially about accountability. Every law, by which someone may be held guilty of legally unacceptable fault, must be accompanied by mechanisms by which the wrongdoer can be held to account. That mechanism must be clearly defined and capable of being understood and put to use by those it affects – both accuser and accused. Most of all, the fact that law is about calling wrongdoers to account to their victims should provide the sole basis for defining what is legally wrong. The 'victims' may be individuals or society itself may be the victim but there is no point in creating law without accountability for its breach.

The business of setting professional standards of conduct is different. It is something which extends beyond the narrow confines of law and penalty. The setting of these standards is part of the process by which a profession aspires to its own professional excellence. It is a job for the teaching profession to be undertaken with confidence in partnership with the consumers and managers of education. These issues are discussed in more detail in the following chapter, 'Cracking the code: The practicalities of managing and regulating professional conduct'.

Chapter 5

Cracking the code

The practicalities of managing and regulating professional conduct

David James

This chapter explores some of the challenges which arise for school leaders and managers in handling the conduct and behaviour of staff in schools. It deals with the procedures that apply at individual school level, on the part of the employer and at national level. The aim is to give school leaders a sense of what may be required of them in managing staff conduct issues and how their actions fit into the wider perspective of how the profession is regulated nationally. In the course of describing these practicalities, it recognises that ethical dilemmas may lie at the heart of many of the issues school leaders face.

General background: the context of the school

One theme of this book is that decisions about whether certain forms of behaviour are acceptable or not are notoriously difficult. Each case raises unique issues and there are often differences of response depending upon people's age, experience, religion and belief. What may be acceptable in private life may not be acceptable in working life. Further complexities are overlain where those concerned are working with children and young people. The issues are particularly complex, where sexuality is the centre of concern.

Heads and governors are all too aware of the importance of the place of the school in the community. The inter-relationships between schools and their local community are complex. In some schools, a problem with one member of staff may have a disproportionate impact: for example in a two-teacher school. But even in a large institution, an apparently small personnel problem, if unattended, may spiral into gossip and misinformation, sucking in staff and spreading disquiet into the community beyond.

Heads and governors share the responsibility of establishing and maintaining the school's ethos in consultation with parents and staff. Having to deal with the myriad problems that arise in schools on a daily basis, they must retain a focus on the wider picture – the good running of the school, the interests of pupils, and still wider obligations to the community. In the midst of daily school life, a complex personnel problem, especially one requiring difficult moral judgements, will not be welcome. And because, like the proverbial bus, problems never come on their own, they will always coincide with at least two other major crises which require urgent attention.

Although the principle of teachers acting in *loco parentis* may be now in question, (see chapter 4) the issue of trust is still a priority. Parents trust teachers to safeguard the best interests of the children in their care.

Under employment legislation, employers trust employees to give 'faithful service'. In return employees trust employers to take reasonable care of their interests, including their health and safety. The role of the trade unions and professional associations in supporting employees is also vital. Their co-operation can be essential in helping to resolve difficult issues.

The overall framework of conditions of service relating to teacher employment is made up of contractual provisions enshrined in the Conditions of Employment of School Teachers ('The Burgundy Book') and the School Teachers' Pay and Conditions Document. The latter particularly, with its list of 29 statutory duties required of teachers, is essential reading for school leaders in England and Wales.

Since 1998, the responsibilities for staffing matters in schools have been shared between the headteacher and the governing body under the provisions of the Education Reform Act 1998. Under this Act the governing body has had the responsibility for determining dismissal and appeal decisions, with the headteacher normally making a recommendation for action. And whilst these arrangements may continue, the effect of the School Staffing (England) Regulations 2003 was, from 1 September 2003, potentially to place a greater level of responsibility upon the headteacher in determining the initial decision as to whether staff should be dismissed, leaving the governors to determine any appeal.

Guidance to staff: codes of conduct

Acting as guidance to staff about expected standards of conduct and also as a yardstick for school leaders to measure misconduct, most LEAs now have a code of conduct for staff in schools (see chapter 6). Other sectors may have equivalent codes setting out minimum acceptable standards of conduct.

Such a code will usually include a disclaimer to the effect that it is not exhaustive and cannot cover all eventualities. It is, however, likely to cover:

- interaction with pupils, including the use of appropriate language and teaching materials;
- arrangements for meetings with pupils, particularly on a one-to-one basis, or on sensitive matters;
- the position with respect to physical contact, particularly with special needs and vulnerable children;
- the legal position relating to corporal punishment;
- the disclosure of confidential information about the school and its pupils;
- the use of the school and LEA's property;
- acceptance of gifts, loans, fees, hospitality;
- conflict of interest, in making appointments and other arrangements;
- the possible impact of the teacher undertaking activities outside work, whether or not they relate to the teaching role and involve payment.

The code is likely to say that failure to observe its provisions may be taken into account in considering action under disciplinary procedures, whilst confirming that should this occur, full consideration will be given to all the facts and circumstances. Because a code of conduct can never cover all eventualities, the framing of the document is likely to be generalised and illustrative, acknowledging the responsibility of the individual teacher to exercise professional judgement in relation to their actions. It is not, of course, the role of a code of conduct to substitute for professional judgement. Its function should, rather, be seen as the means of providing clarity and consistency across the school and the school system.

It is worth noting here, though, that whilst such codes will normally cover relationships between teachers and their pupils, it is less common to find references to the implications of such relationships between colleagues on the staff. Such codes are also, increasingly, recognising the potential for misconduct arising from electronic forms of communication, including the internet, email, mobile phones and text messaging.

Professional standards and professional judgement

The exercise of judgement by the individual teacher is the hallmark of professionalism. But the relationship between the individual teacher responsible for exercising professional judgement, and external statements of professional standards, ethics and values is not always a comfortable one. One commentator, Ian Stronach, has identified a tension between what he terms 'inside-out' professionalism, based on the individual judgement of the practitioner, and 'outside-in' professionalism, made up of an increasingly overbearing superstructure of externally prescribed standards, targets and competencies. He suggests that teachers in taking day-to-day decisions operate within a tension, continually torn by dilemmas and compromises. And professionalism, arguably, cannot be professionalism if it is a comfortable state of moral certainty. Surely it is part of a professional's lot to be engaged in a continuous process of internal dialogue, in which day-to-day problems are continually tested against a sense of standards and principles, which are then revised and internalised in the light of experience.

But if standards may be open to differing interpretations, most people would agree that internal coherence in individual behaviour is vital: in other words, that aligning what we say, what we do and what we are is the basis of moral standing.

On this subject, the literature of teachers and teaching is littered with examples of the moral hypocrisy which flouts such consistency: indeed, it might be tempting to think that this is the dominant theme in the portrayal of the profession! To name but a few there are Thwackham and Square in *Tom Jones*, pillars of rectitude, caught with their trousers down; Gradgrind in *Hard Times* whose high handed utilitarianism is exposed as lacking humanity and Wackford Sqeers in *Nicholas Nickleby* who eventually answers for monstrous ill treatment of pupils. Perhaps the modern day equivalent is the errant and pressurised profession depicted in Channel 4's *Teachers*. Am I alone in thinking there are not quite so many shining examples of moral rectitude and pedagogical inspiration within the literature of teaching?

It is hardly surprising that personnel matters, especially those raising complex moral and ethical issues, have the capacity to test school managers and leaders in ways which other aspects of school life don't quite do. Staffing issues somehow have the ability to call into question one's *own* values and test one's *own* sense of internal moral consistency. It is never easy to discipline a colleague for a lapse one may have committed oneself, even if that was some time ago. Possession of cannabis is the example which most readily comes to mind. Dealing with such issues may bring our whole lives into focus: we may, indeed, have to confront our youthful selves in carrying out the responsibilities of our adult selves. The issues which can arise are almost endlessly varied as described earlier in the book.

As a head, what do you do if:

- your deputy starts an affair with the new school secretary?
- you are told two female members of staff are kissing in the playground?
- a young member of staff is arrested outside a nightclub with a dozen ecstasy tablets?
- a female member of staff tells you they are undergoing gender reassignment and has discussed it within the PHSE programme?
- you learn that a teacher has taken a 15-year-old pupil in as a lodger?
- a newly qualified teacher (NQT) has sent soft toys and flowers to a sixth former?

Some school leaders have been tempted to bury their heads in the sand!

Dealing with difficult issues: initial assessment

Initial advice to any headteacher faced with issues like these is to step back and assess the situation. This will usually reveal that the information to hand is only partial: that you need a systematic enquiry to find out all the relevant facts and circumstances. In the case above involving the deputy head, there will be many things you might need to know. What is the nature of the relationship? How long has it been going on? Is it public knowledge? Who else is involved/affected? Have any incidents taken place on the school premises? Are there personal circumstances, such as health or other factors, which may be relevant? Has he been under stress or been behaving erratically? Has she? *The most important single factor, however, will be whether the relationship is impacting adversely upon the school and affecting the trust and confidence you can have in these staff, considered as employees, to carry out their duties within the school.* If not, the matter should be consigned to the realm of their private affairs. Though it may be tempting to try to manage everything which might impinge on school, there are dangers in over managing. Boundaries need to be established and it is important to remember that the reach of the employer's responsibility does not extend haphazardly and invariably into the private life of its employees.

So stage one must always be a dispassionate assessment of what is known from:

- colleagues;
- pupils;
- parents;
- governors;
- an outside agency;
- members of the public;
- the police;
- the press.

It will help initially to form a picture of what kind of issue you are dealing with and define it.

- Is it apparent misconduct?
- Is it apparent incompetence?
- Does it relate to the employee's health or private life?
- Is it a combination of some or all of these things?

It may come to you in the form of an allegation, a complaint or simply 'information' passed on by someone without understanding its significance. It may appear trivial and in fact be serious or vice versa. You may instinctively feel the source is unreliable – perhaps from a parent with a long history of vexatious complaint against the school – but care should be taken not to ignore them simply on that basis.

If the issue is potentially serious it is likely that you will wish to seek immediate advice from a personnel or legal adviser, usually in the Local Education Authority (or, if the school is outside the maintained sector, another legal or personnel adviser). Hopefully there will be a relationship of trust and confidence which will allow such advice to be sought and confidently acted upon.

Minor issues: advice and counselling

There will be plenty of occasions where formal disciplinary action is neither appropriate nor necessary and where the matter is better dealt with informally, through giving advice, as part of general management responsibilities. This might include drawing the individual's attention to the relevant provisions of the code of conduct or their conditions of service. This advice may be oral but unless the issue is very minor, it is good practice to write it down so that there is a record of what has been said. This is a prime example of where professional judgement and a sense of proportion are essential to the successful management and leadership of other professionals.

Informal advice and counselling are likely to be particularly appropriate with newly qualified staff, whether these are young or mature entrants, whose sense of the standards and ethos of the profession may still be in development. This general aspect of teacher professionalism has been most recently recognised in the revision of the national standards for the award of qualified teacher status (QTS) which now contain a section on professional values and practice. This states that those awarded QTS must understand and uphold the Code of Professional Values and Practice of the General Teaching Council (GTC) for England by demonstrating and promoting 'the positive values, attitudes and behaviour that they expect from their pupils' and 'are aware of and work within, the statutory frameworks relating to teachers' responsibilities'.

The induction standards which apply to the first year of professional practice in the maintained sector, require the new teacher to continue to meet the qualified teacher status (QTS) standards in the context of employment as a qualified teacher: to, in effect, put them into practice in the real context of the school. Teachers who do not meet these standards may fail their induction year. (If they do, they may appeal, in England, to its General Teaching Council.)

Thus, if it is reported that a young teacher has been seen drinking and flirting with sixth formers in the pub, you would probably wish to see them to offer advice. You would not be so sympathetic with a longstanding member of staff, who in your opinion, really should know better, particularly if there were other worrying symptoms which caused you to doubt their judgement or motivation. Such activities are increasingly understood within the context of 'grooming', though, as ever, the issue must be approached with an open mind.

Major issues: can the member of staff remain in school?

At the other end of the scale, an issue, which *will arise* in the most serious cases, is whether the member of staff can be allowed to remain on the school premises. This will occur where there is an issue of apparent gross misconduct or where the continued presence of the employee could interfere with an investigation through contact with witnesses or evidence. In other words, should you take the serious and always traumatic step of suspending the individual?

Prima facie gross misconduct, which can justify suspension, will probably be defined within the code of conduct and is likely to include issues such as:

- sexual misconduct, with pupils or adults;
- physical assault;
- fraud;
- malicious damage;
- misconduct relating to examinations;
- misrepresentation;
- criminal offences.

Such conduct may arise within or beyond the school. Misconduct beyond the school can be assessed in terms of whether it has brought the school into disrepute. This issue is again relevant to the trust and confidence which the employer can have in the employee to fulfil their professional role and their ability to comply with the terms of their contract. Some employers specify 'bringing the employer's name into disrepute' as an instance of gross misconduct warranting dismissal within their codes or other workplace rules. However, if the employer does rely on this, it will important to be able to make the case for the alleged impact on the performance of the job. An employer may also be justified in treating a senior employee more severely than a junior employee because of the increased level of responsibility held and the greater potential for disrepute this entails: this might be a factor in addressing, for instance, the publicly visible misconduct of a senior member of staff, particularly if they had a high profile role, such as responsibility for community and parental liaison. By definition, it might also be a factor in assessing the appropriate response in relation to misconduct by the headteacher, him or herself. Such an assessment can legitimately include the impact of any press coverage.

Allegations of abuse

A particular area of focus in recent of years has been the management of situations in which school staff are accused of the physical or sexual abuse of pupils. These situations are among the most complex, testing and traumatic for any school leader to face (see chapter 6 for a first-hand account). Fortunately, in England, extensive guidance has been provided by the Council of Local Education Authorities (CLEA) in their publication *Teachers Facing an Allegation of Physical/sexual Abuse: Guidance on Practice and Procedure*, produced in May 1995, amended in 1997 and incorporated within DfES Circular 10/95 *Protecting Children from Abuse: The Role of the Education Service*.

This guidance should by now be well established in the practice of local authorities as well as being the subject of awareness raising with heads and governors. Where such an issue does arise, co-ordination of activities is paramount and there is now a network of regional co-ordinators working to ensure that the relevant agencies – police, social services and education – act without delay in a considered and co-ordinated way. Under the Green Paper *Every Child Matters* (2003), co-ordination of activity between agencies concerned with child well-being will be further strengthened through radical proposals for the restructuring of services supporting education and children's social services.

But whether the issue relates to the physical/sexual abuse of children or not, it may be necessary to make urgent arrangements to suspend the member of staff to enable the matter to be investigated. Whether the person is 'guilty' or not, suspension is always traumatic, even life-changing, for the individual concerned (see chapter 3). The head's job is to manage this unenviable task as professionally as possible. Where the issue relates to the head, a member of the governing body will normally be designated to take action, in consultation with a personnel adviser.

If it is necessary to suspend, it is good practice to allow the individual to be accompanied by a trade union representative or a friend, to provide advice and support, both during the interview and after it and to rehearse the facts briefly, giving opportunity for response before reaching a decision.

If the decision is to suspend, the individual should be informed orally and given written confirmation as soon as possible. Where the issue is one of child abuse, the relevant procedures provide for a joint strategy discussion to take place with the police and/or social services (as appropriate) before deciding what action to take.

At the meeting, which will always be a tense affair, it should be explained that suspension is in itself not a disciplinary measure, and is carried out without prejudice, to enable the matter to be investigated fairly and objectively.

Written confirmation should follow as soon as possible, to:

- confirm that the individual should not come onto school premises;
- explain any relevant terms of the suspension, such as return of school property, contact with pupils or staff;
- give a contact point for information during the suspension;
- provide the opportunity for independent and impartial counselling.

The need for investigation

Whether suspension is required or not, the next step will be to undertake a full and fair investigation into the matters of concern by appointing an investigating officer. (*Note*: in child protection cases this role may be taken by the police/social services. If so, the school should stand aside from the investigation and co-operate fully with the process.)

The appointment of a fair and thorough investigating officer is vital to the whole process. This could either be a senior member of the school staff (perhaps a deputy head or another member of the leadership group) or a person external to the school such as an LEA officer. The investigating officer needs tact, diplomacy, firmness and the ability to ask the right questions. Where children need to be questioned, parents should be notified, either so that they can be present or to agree the presence of another member of staff.

In some circumstances, it may be necessary to commission a report by an external expert such as an auditor, a computer consultant or a handwriting expert. In this case, it is always important to agree the basis on which the report will be produced and the timescale.

Collecting all the information and collating a covering report is not an easy task, particularly when there are pressures to complete the job quickly. The success of the entire disciplinary process will depend on an accurate, thorough and fair report at this stage.

Communication issues

Issues relating to staff (especially scandalous ones) do not normally remain secret for long. No one who has worked in a school will underestimate the power of the grapevine! Where information has leaked out, a carefully planned core statement should be prepared and a decision taken about whether to send an appropriate version to

- staff;
- pupils;
- parents;
- governors;
- others, including potentially the media.

The guiding principle will be 'the need to know'.

Not all situations require the world at large to know that Mr or Ms X has been suspended pending enquiries, though in some cases where the matter has become already well known, including outside the school, this might be unavoidable. Whilst it is important that the true situation is not misrepresented, in some circumstances, it will be possible, and true, to say that Mr/Ms X is absent from school on sick leave. It is desirable to agree the line to be taken with the teacher concerned and any representative they may have. The LEA and, in the case of denominational schools, the diocese, will also be able to assist.

Deciding upon the case: the disciplinary interview

The role of the investigating officer is to produce a fair and objective report, setting out the evidence in a balanced way, in order that a decision can be made as to whether there is a case to answer at a formal disciplinary interview. The role of the 'interviewing officer' (normally the headteacher) is to hear the evidence, question the parties, and reach a decision on the facts, whether the facts amount to misconduct and, if so, whether a disciplinary sanction is appropriate. A formal disciplinary interview convened under the school's disciplinary procedure, is likely to provide for a structured process, with timescales, whereby:

- the investigating officer presents the case;
- the teacher and representative have the right of reply;
- there is opportunity for questioning by the interviewing officer at either stage;
- the investigating officer sums up;
- the teacher/representative sum up;
- a decision is made.

Careful thought should be given to the venue: normally it may well be appropriate to hold the hearing offsite on 'neutral ground'. Once the process is complete, the decision of the interviewing officer may be to take no disciplinary action, or to issue

- a formal oral warning;
- a formal written warning;
- a final written warning;
- a recommendation for dismissal.

These decisions are based on the 'balance of probabilities': in other words, by weighing up the evidence on a common sense basis and reaching a reasonable judgement about what to do. It should be remembered, though, that this is not a court of law where decisions are made 'beyond all reasonable doubt'. Managers taking action under employment procedures are not expected to be judges in a court of law and the onus on them is to come to a reasonable judgement in all the circumstances.

Because disciplinary situations are always complex and testing, the process should never be rushed. Time must always be set aside to consider the case in a measured and thoughtful way and reach a considered conclusion. If it is not possible to conclude the case in a single day, it may be necessary to reconvene on another day, despite the inconvenience this may cause.

The purposes of disciplinary action

Up to the stage of dismissal, the purposes of disciplinary action are

- to alert the teacher to the fact that their conduct is unsatisfactory;
- to state the consequences if it does not improve;
- to formalise any actions required by the teacher;
- to explain any support measures which may be necessary.

It would be wrong to suggest that disciplinary action does not involve an element of punishment: indeed if dismissal of the employee follows, this conclusion is inescapable. However, it should be remembered that up until the dismissal stage punishment is not the purpose of disciplinary action and it is expected that the employer will take a constructive approach which is focused on improvement.

It is interesting to place the principles applying to the discipline of pupils alongside those applying to staff. Where pupils are concerned most would agree that you should:

- make it clear you are addressing behaviour and not them personally;
- be specific about the causes of concern;
- address the issue as close as possible to the point of origin (in other words, do not store up a range of concerns);
- be firm, consistent and fair;
- be constructive and clear about what needs to be done to improve.

The issue of proportionality in decision making is vital: there should be no overreaction or shooting from the hip. This principle was well expressed by Lord Denning, who stated that such decisions by employers should fall within 'a band of reasonable responses'. The disciplinary response, in other words, must be proportionate – you do not dismiss an employee for one small lapse after years of good and loyal service.

In addition, there will be the need to allow for the possibility of appeal before an independent panel of governors and to communicate the outcome to any complainant, to staff, parents, governors, pupils, the community and the media, as necessary and appropriate.

Health issues

The course of disciplinary investigations and hearings is seldom straightforward. Along the way, there may be discussions with trade union representatives, frustrations and delays. And frequently, proceedings will be interrupted by the stress and ill health of the teacher concerned. Where this occurs, the employer will be well advised to seek an expert view, usually from an occupational health adviser, probably based in the local authority, who will be able to advise on the effect of the person's ill health on their capacity to attend for work, including their fitness to take part in disciplinary proceedings.

In managing these processes, it is always important to keep the management of the disciplinary issue distinct from the issue of managing attendance and to be prepared that capability procedures relating to ill health may, in some circumstances, supersede the disciplinary process.

Issues beyond employment: challenges

Where the employee has been dismissed, there may still arise the possibility of challenge at employment tribunal and even beyond that at employment appeal tribunal. These challenges relate to the fairness or otherwise of the dismissal (or, in the case of constructive dismissal, the resignation) and will address alleged unfairness in employers' procedures. In some circumstances, it may be appropriate to seek to settle the issue through a legally binding compromise agreement, whereby the employee agrees to resign and waive certain statutory rights in return for a severance payment. Personnel and legal advice should always be sought if this is felt necessary or desirable.

Reference has been made in the previous chapter to the fact that decisions previously made with reasonable consistency across 104 LEAs are now made by 25,000 heads and governing bodies. Whilst this has certainly had the intended effect of devolving responsibility to the 'front line' and increasing 'ownership' of this key area of school management, it also places renewed emphasis on the need for objectivity and fairness on the part of those who are, by definition, much closer to the issues. Greater autonomy brings greater responsibility and, in turn, emphasises the need to act with appropriate personnel and legal advice.

At the heart of the matter, inescapably, is the decision as to whether certain facts amount to misconduct and merit a disciplinary sanction. There are no easy answers to this fundamental question: as Graham Clayton has commented in chapter 4, 'there is no commonly understood definition of a badly behaving teacher'. Like any quasi-judicial decision, this is a matter of judgement, informed where possible by a code of conduct and *taking account of* (but not being bound by) any precedent which may exist (the LEA may be helpful here). Inevitably, the exercise of this judgement will involve the sometimes agonising internal dialogue about moral principles referred to earlier: but the process must always be about considering *this* set of facts and *this* set of mitigating circumstances against expected standards of behaviour. Professional judgement is required – not to mention, at times, the wisdom of Solomon.

Let us say that you have addressed the issue of the school deputy and secretary referred to earlier. You find that there has been indiscretion on both their parts: they have kissed and cuddled and reportedly fondled each other. This has been on school premises, in the sports hall, after school hours. It has not been witnessed by pupils although this is fortuitous since pupils were in the vicinity. There is some debate about whether they have engaged in 'heavy petting' but opinions are divided as to what this means. You have debated whether their actions merit a formal written warning or a final written warning. You have also debated whether they merit the same sanction or whether there is scope for differentiation, given the deputy seems to have 'led the way'. After further thought, however, you consider 'it takes two to tango'. They are both contrite and refer to various personal pressures and difficulties. The Code of Conduct speaks of the need for staff to uphold high standards of personal conduct. You decide to be lenient, treat the incident as a 'one off' and give each of them a formal written warning. They do not appeal. Your chair of governors then asks to see you and complains you've been 'soft' – he also wants to take the matter further . . . Your conclusion is 'you can't win'!

Prevention rather than cure

It would be wrong to conclude this section on employer responses without pointing out the fact that, in managing misconduct, prevention is better than cure. Whilst school leaders may at any time be on the receiving end of a staff misconduct crisis, there is much that can and should be done to raise awareness of key issues and forestall such issues from arising in the first place. But whilst much time is spent inculcating expected standards of behaviour amongst pupils, less, if any, may be spent on expected standards of staff behaviour (outside obvious child protection concerns).

An awareness-raising session based upon a discussion of the LEA's or school's Code of Conduct will be time well spent in clarifying issues and providing reassurance. The debate is likely to be lively, and all the better for it!

The role of regulatory bodies

Employer procedures do not, of course, in themselves determine the ability of the teacher to continue to practise their profession. For many years the province of the Department of Education and Skills, this role is now shared with the recently established General Teaching Councils for England, Wales and Northern Ireland as well as the General Teaching Council for Scotland established in 1965.

The Department for Education and Skills (DfES)

The Secretary of State for Education and Skills has longstanding powers to determine the fitness of teachers and others to continue to work with children and young people under the age of 19. These are now set out in the *Education (Prohibition from Teaching or Working with Children) Regulations 2003* and the accompanying guidance document *Child Protection: Procedures for Barring or Restricting People Working with Children in Education* (July 2003).

The process of consideration by the Secretary of State involves the referral of cases relating to teachers where their employers have decided to dispense with their services for reasons of misconduct or where the teacher has resigned before this stage. Employers should report such cases within one month of the teacher ceasing employment. Cases considered by the Secretary of State also include teachers convicted of criminal offences by the courts.

There are certain very serious categories of sexual offences against children where barring is automatic. In other cases, officials hold a confidential interview with the teacher to gather the facts before referring the case to a minister for decision.

Teachers can be restricted from working with children and young people partially or completely. These proceedings are held in private although under human rights legislation, the teacher may appeal to a Care Standards Tribunal against a decision to bar them from employment. Barred teachers are placed on the Register of Persons Considered Unsuitable to Work with Children, previously the Department's List 99.

The DfES guidance explains that:

> There is not a comprehensive definition of the kind of behaviour that will lead the Secretary of State to consider making a direction but, broadly speaking, it includes:
>
> a. violent behaviour towards children or young people
> b. behaviour, which involves a breach of a teacher's position of trust, such as a sexual, or otherwise inappropriate, relationship with a pupil (regardless of whether the pupil is over the age of consent)
> c. a sexual offence against someone over the age of 16
> d. behaviour which indicates a risk to others
> e. any offence involving serious violence
> f. drug trafficking and other drug related offences
> g. stealing school property or monies
> h. deception in relation to employment as a teacher, or at a school or further education institution, for example false claims about qualifications, or failure to disclose past convictions
> i. a criminal conviction which results in a sentence of more than 12 months imprisonment
> j. behaviour which could lead to prosecution for a criminal offence
> k. repeated misconduct or multiple convictions, unless of a very minor nature
> l. behaviour, which involves a breach of the standards of propriety expected of the teaching profession, such as falsifying pupil records, or assisting pupils to cheat or gain unfair advantage in examinations.

It should also be noted that: 'A person's sexual orientation or private sexual behaviour is not grounds for considering barring them, unless it raises questions about the safety or welfare of children or others.'

From 1 June 2001, the DfES has referred cases which do not raise concerns about the safety and welfare of children and young persons under the age of 19 to the General Teaching Councils for England and Wales.

It remains the responsibility of employers at the time of making appointments, to check the suitability of teachers and others seeking to work with children and young people against the department's Register as well as to check their criminal background. Since 2001 these checks are undertaken through the Criminal Records Bureau (CRB).

The General Teaching Councils

In September 2000, parliament established General Teaching Councils for England and Wales, a General Teaching Council for Scotland having been established in 1965. The Councils for England and Wales were established with two aims:

- to contribute to improving the standards of teaching and the quality of learning;
- to maintain and improve standards of conduct amongst teachers.

Both aims are to be carried out in the interests of the public.

The concept behind the Councils' regulatory role is that of 'professionally-led self regulation'. This marks a fundamental shift of approach from a regime based on regulation through government and the Civil Service. The basis of this system is that members of the profession are themselves entrusted to regulate the misconduct and incompetence of their fellow members and to determine whether and on what terms they should remain in the profession. This is therefore not a 'top-down' but essentially a 'peer assessment' approach, trusting the profession to set and regulate the standards of conduct (and competence) of its own members. The principles date back to the self-regulating craftsmen guilds of past centuries.

In practice, most professional self-regulatory bodies have statutory provisions, which provide for the inclusion of a lay element in the committees deciding cases in order to guard against any charges of cronyism and to provide for an informed external input. The General Teaching Council for England is the example taken here.

In terms of receiving cases, the Council may receive a complaint about a teacher's conduct from employers, from members of the public or through the notification of a criminal offence by the courts. All employer-referred conduct cases are referred initially to the DfES who deal with them if they raise child protection concerns. In terms of complaints about a teacher's competence (which is not the issue here) the Council may only receive a referral from an employer where the employer has ceased to use the teacher's services or the teacher has ceased to provide those services for reasons of incompetence.

Employer referred cases are considered, firstly, by an investigating committee of Council members who decide whether there is 'a case to answer'. If so, the case is referred to either a professional conduct committee or, where relevant, a professional competence committee of Council members.

Because the decisions of the regulatory body affect the right of an individual to practise their profession, thereby determining a civil right, all proceedings of disciplinary committees fall under Article 6 of the Human Rights Act. This requirement means that the teacher has a right to 'a fair and public hearing within a reasonable time before an independent and impartial tribunal'. Every element of this legal requirement is represented in the way the Council carries out its regulatory role and is embodied in the Council's Disciplinary Rules of Procedure.

The role of the hearing committee is to decide whether the teacher is guilty of 'Unacceptable Professional Conduct' or 'Serious Professional Incompetence'. The definitions of these terms are contained in the Rules as follows:

- 'Unacceptable professional conduct' means conduct which falls short of the standard expected of a registered teacher within the meaning of paragraph 8 (1) of Schedule 2 to the (Teaching and Higher Education Act 1998) and is behaviour which involves a breach of the standards of propriety expected of the profession.
- 'Serious professional incompetence' means demonstrating a level of competence which falls seriously short of that expected of a registered teacher.

Essential to the decision-making process on individual cases is a thorough and objective consideration of the facts according to a staged decision-making procedure whereby each committee:

- determines whether the facts are proved;
- determines whether the facts amount to 'Unacceptable Professional Conduct' or 'Serious Professional Incompetence';
- considers the teacher's history and character and any mitigating circumstances;
- determines whether to make a disciplinary order in terms of the teacher's eligibility for registration.

The orders available are:

- a reprimand (which remains on the register for a two-year period);
- a conditional registration order (allowing the teacher to continue to practise subject to meeting certain conditions);
- a suspension order (for up to two years, and to which conditions may be attached);
- a prohibition order, (removing eligibility to register subject to reapplication in a period of not less than two years).

Teachers have a right of appeal to the High Court which has wide ranging powers to review the process and annul or redetermine the case.

The Councils' job, of course, is distinct from that of the employer and is to determine the teacher's 'registrability' rather than their 'employability': i.e. their ability to remain registered with the Council and to practise their profession in maintained schools and non-maintained special schools in England as opposed to their employment in a particular post. Under the Education Act 2002, cases are normally considered by the Council where an employer 'has ceased to use the services' of a teacher or where the employer 'might have ceased to use those services had the teacher not ceased to provide them', although there is provision for members of the public and parents to make a misconduct allegation.

Thus, without a dismissal or resignation, the case of the deputy head, referred to earlier, would not be referred to the Secretary of State (and on to the Council). However, it is possible that a disgruntled party (even the chair of governors) could make such an allegation direct to the Council.

An important principle in the work of both the DfES and the GTC is that the standards of propriety expected of the profession extend within and beyond the school or educational setting in which the individual works. Like doctors, nurses and lawyers, teachers are expected to recognise the implications of their professional status in society. Professionalism, in this sense, does not end at the school gate.

Although this is sometimes a matter of concern, the issue of professional judgement should not be confused with arguments about 'never being off duty' or the fact that teachers are expected to be moral paragons. There is a reasonable balance to be struck – the common denominator is professional judgement. And just as the employer can take into account the impact of the employee's actions on the employer's reputation, the Council can and does consider the impact of the teacher's actions on the reputation of the profession.

As previously pointed out, media portrayals of the teaching profession are often less than flattering. And against a background of generally high professional standards, there is plenty of evidence that teachers do not welcome negative portrayals of their professionalism:

Broadcasters and TV programme makers were criticised by teachers yesterday for portraying them in soaps and dramas as heavy drinking, lazy, dishonest and irresponsible.

Programmes like BBC1's *Hope and Glory* and Channel 4's *Teachers* were pointed out for showing negative images of schools and the people who worked in them, with promiscuous sexual behaviour and drug taking presented as the norm.

Delegates attending the annual conference of the Professional Association of Teachers in Cardiff complained that such programmes were putting teachers in a bad light and sending out the wrong message to youngsters who were heavily influenced by television.

Teachers were important role models for children, but the way television presented them was bringing their profession into disrepute.

(*Guardian Unlimited*, 3 August 2001)

Self-regulation, such as applies to doctors through the General Medical Council, to solicitors through the Law Society and to nurses and midwives through the Nursing and Midwifery Council, accepts and builds on the principle of professional responsibility illustrated here. For this reason, it is often seen as a privilege rather than a right since it places the professions in a position of high trust as the guardian of their own professional standards. Hearing committees of the Council, always comprising a majority of practising teachers, bring their knowledge of the profession and sense of judgement about professional standards to decisions about the small number of their peers who come before them. The Council assumed its regulatory responsibilities in June 2001, held its first investigating committee in October 2001 and its first disciplinary hearing in March 2002.

One consequence of this system is that for the first time the misconduct and serious professional incompetence of teachers is open to public scrutiny. Members of the public and the press may attend disciplinary hearings of the Council and the press regularly choose to do so. (It should be noted that a committee may exclude the public where there are exceptional reasons relating to the interests of justice or the protection of children or third parties).

Disciplinary experience so far

At the time of writing, the GTC for England has heard fifty cases of misconduct across the following range:

- inappropriate language and/or inappropriate conduct in respect of pupils;
- actions which undermine the school and/or colleagues;
- misconduct relating to the management and administration of examinations and assessment arrangements;
- fraud and financial impropriety;
- misrepresentation of qualifications and other matters;
- misconduct relating to contractual matters;
- misconduct outside the workplace including criminal convictions.

These have included cases where:

- a teacher undermined colleagues by mischievously disclosing information relating to threshold assessment;

- a teacher was convicted of indecent assault of a colleague and being drunk on an aircraft during a school trip;
- a teacher was convicted of harassment of his estranged wife out of school;
- two teachers accessed pornography on the internet using school computers.

The GTC has used the full range of its sanctions in addressing these issues and has reported in summary form on its disciplinary experience in its Registrar's annual report. Cases are also regularly reported in the *Times Educational Supplement*.

An important priority for the Council is not merely to regulate the profession but to feed back to employers and the profession the fruits of this experience so that it may lead to greater awareness and improved practice. The Registrar's annual report, available on the Council's website, includes an 'issues arising' section drawing attention to what may be learned.

In the spirit of constructive rather than punitive discipline, the Council is researching more and better ways to remedy poor conduct and competence through the use of conditional registration orders.

And although there are some differences between the context within which employers and regulators operate – not least the significantly different legal frameworks which apply – there are many similarities, particularly a common interest in ensuring high standards of conduct and behaviour and the enduring importance of professional judgement.

National codes of conduct

Many regulatory bodies consider it important to develop a professional code of conduct to seek to ensure that:

- individual practitioners are clear about expected standards of conduct;
- those standards are transparent to the public;
- the regulatory body has a clear set of expectations for use in reaching disciplinary decisions.

These bodies may also develop codes of practice, codes of values or codes of ethics explaining the underlying basis of expectations upon the profession.

Like codes produced by employers, these documents cannot be an exhaustive catalogue of the types of conduct or performance which may be deemed unacceptable, although they will provide guidance to decision makers.

But this work needs to be seen in context. It is possible to understand the territory of professional standards in three dimensions:

- promoting and inspiring high standards;
- defining and ensuring acceptable standards;
- defining and regulating unacceptable standards.

The Council, having been set up in 2000, needed to orientate itself in relation to these dimensions. Whilst it might have been possible for the Council to produce, first off, a code in the third area, a decision was made that to do so would contribute unhelpfully to the superstructure of external prescription – the 'outside in professionalism' referred to earlier and that a more positive first step was preferable. Accordingly, the Council led off with a code which addressed the first dimension. The Code of Professional Values and Practice for Teachers, produced in 2002, 'confirms and celebrates the high standards of teachers' professional practice in this country and describes the professional values which underpin that practice'.

The Council developed this code through an unprecedented process of consultation, exploring the concept with teachers in meetings nationwide before consulting all registered teachers in England (*c.* 500,000) on the draft. There were 20,000 responses, with 77 per cent affirming the content. The aim was to create an expression of professional standards generated and owned by the profession, which emphasises the knowledge, beliefs and attitudes which underlie teacher professionalism.

The Code of Values and Practice contains important paragraphs which bear upon relationships between adults. There is, for instance, a section on Teacher Colleagues, which states:

> Teachers respect the rights of other people to equal opportunities and to dignity at work.
>
> (GTC, 2002)

The code also recognises the point made earlier about conduct within and beyond the school gate:

Teachers support the place of the school in the community and appreciate the importance of their own professional status in society. They recognise that professionalism involves using judgement over appropriate standards of personal behaviour.

(GTC, 2002)

Aside from an expression of values, beliefs and attitudes, there is still a place for the expression of standards for use within the regulatory regime: in other words, a code in the third area above. To this end, the Council has developed a code of conduct drawing on the experience of its findings in disciplinary hearings. Through this code, the profession, acting through the Council as the professional body, has taken the opportunity to set out the minimum acceptable standards of conduct and behaviour which are expected of its members and which will be taken into account in reaching decisions on individual cases.

The underlying ethical debate

In the context of the ethical issues referred to in this chapter, it is significant to note that one paragraph of the Code of Professional Values and Practice, that on equal opportunities, caused the greatest debate during the extensive consultation process which the Council undertook with the profession and partner groups. If ever one was needed, this provided a telling reminder of how closely below the surface lie those raw issues of ethics and values which underpin professional life and of the passionate way in which opposing views are held. The draft code had read:

Teachers recognise diversity and work to ensure the rights of individuals to develop. They fully respect differences of gender, marital status, religion, colour, race, ethnicity, sexual orientation and disability. Teacher professionalism involves challenging prejudice and stereotypes to ensure equality of opportunity.

(GTC, 2001)

The appearance of the consultation version led to the publication of a leaflet by an organisation called the Christian Institute, with the headline:

Cut the clause – Teachers should not have to promote gay rights – Why clause 5 of the draft professional code should be scrapped July 2001

(Christian Institute, 2001)

The leaflet went on to state:

In clause 5 of the code the GTC has decided to go well beyond equal opportunities. Under this Clause teachers become both the promoters of rights, including gay rights, and the challengers of stereotyping. It is not enough to treat all pupils impartially. It is not enough to fully respect young people as people. Now teachers must fully respect differences based on sexual orientation.

(Christian Institute, 2001)

After careful thought, the revised wording of the Code was agreed by Council as follows:

To ensure the positive development of individual pupils, teachers work within a framework of equal opportunities and other relevant legislation, statutory guidance and school policies. Within this framework, teachers challenge stereotypes and oppose prejudice to safeguard equality of opportunity, respecting individuals regardless of gender, marital status, religion, colour, race, ethnicity, class, sexual orientation, disability and age.

(GTC, 2002)

Conclusion

This chapter has described the procedures and processes relating to the professional misconduct of teachers as they arise at employer level and at the level of the bodies regulating the profession: the DfES relating to the safety and welfare of children; the GTC with respect to other forms of misconduct.

What is clear is that whilst general guidance may be given in codes of conduct, both by the employer and by the professional body, this guidance cannot cover every eventuality. The determination of individual cases will always depend upon a thorough consideration of the facts, a sensitive assessment of mitigating circumstances and, above all, the exercise of professional judgement. One thing is certain: no two cases are the same.

Within the employment context, sensitivity and awareness of moral issues will be judged by the employer in terms of the trust and confidence they can continue to place in the employee to continue in their role, including whether the teacher's actions bring the employer into disrepute. In the case of the regulatory body, that decision has the wider framework of whether and on what terms the teacher may continue in the profession, with the interests of the public the prime concern. The basis of such decisions is whether such conduct represents a breach of the standards of propriety expected of the profession, which may include whether it brings the profession into disrepute.

From June 2001, important areas of professional conduct and competence have been subject to decision making by the GTC, bringing the determination and definition of conduct and competence within the conscience of the profession itself. This experience has now informed the development of a code of conduct, which in turn informs decisions about the regulation of members of the profession. It is arguably a sign of a mature profession and, certainly, a mature approach to professional responsibility, that professional judgement has been placed at the centre of a system for ensuring professional standards in this way.

Postscript: future developments for teacher registration and regulation

Since 1 June 2001, teachers, including supply teachers, are required to be registered with the GTC(E) to teach in maintained schools and non-maintained special schools in England. There are a small number of teachers who work in pupil referral units (PRU) who are also covered by this requirement.

The following people are exempt from the requirement to hold QTS and may work in maintained schools or non-maintained special schools, without registration:

- student teachers undertaking initial teacher training (teaching practice);
- teachers working towards QTS through an employment based programme;

- instructors with special qualifications or experience where the school has been unable to find a qualified teacher with the necessary skills and expertise;
- non-EEA (European Economic Area) overseas-trained teachers. These teachers can be employed in temporary posts, either in one school or a number of schools for a total of up to 4 years.

Centrally employed teachers who are teaching in a maintained school or non-maintained special school in England also need to be registered with the GTC(E). Centrally employed staff who do not *teach* in a maintained school or non-maintained special school, do not need to register.

The Council, however, encourages all those with QTS to register voluntarily and this includes, qualified teachers working:

- in independent schools;
- in sixth form colleges;
- otherwise in the further or higher education sectors;
- in outdoor education centres;
- in secure units;
- in nursery schools/classes which are not attached to a school under LEA control;
- solely as home tutors;
- solely as hospital tutors;
- as advisers or consultants who do not take sole control of a class at any time.

Other teachers, including those who are retired and no longer in the teaching profession are also not required to register.

To be eligible to register, a teacher must:

- *Hold qualified teacher status*: i.e. must be a qualified teacher within the meaning of section 218 (2) of the Education Reform Act 1998.
- Not be disqualified from teaching by:

  - the Secretary of State;
  - the GTC(E);
  - an independent schools tribunal; or
  - any of their equivalents in Scotland, Wales and Northern Ireland

- Unless exempt, not have failed to satisfactorily complete an induction period
- From April 2002 pay an annual registration fee.

Issues arising

A number of issues arise from the above arrangements:

1   The requirement to register is based upon employment to teach in particular types of institution – i.e. maintained schools and non-maintained special schools. It is not, in other words, based upon a definition of the clientele – the pupils – who are being taught. This leads to the potential anomaly of a teacher in a maintained school being required to be registered as a condition of employment but a teacher in an outdoor education centre, secure unit or as a home or hospital tutor potentially *teaching the same or more vulnerable pupils*, not being required to be registered.
2   Other groups – those seeking to gain QTS through an employment based programme, instructors with special qualifications or experience, and non-EEA (European Economic Area) overseas-trained teachers teaching in this country for four years – are also currently outside the scope of registration and regulation, albeit engaged in the education of pupils.
3   Eligibilty to register rests upon the possession of qualified teacher status, not being disqualified by the Secretary of State, or the GTCs for England, Scotland, Wales or Northern Ireland and not having failed a statutory induction year. But are there wider factors which should be taken into account before the Council automatically registers a teacher? What of teachers with serious criminal convictions; what of teachers disqualified by the teaching Councils of other countries – Canada or Australia for instance?

The above circumstances are under active consideration by the Council and may lead to further work in partnership with the DfES, in order to:

1   review the basis of compulsory registration for those teaching pupils in a variety of educational settings in the maintained sector;

2   consider arrangements for the provisional registration of trainee
     and overseas qualified teachers;
3   introduce suitability requirements for registration which take
     account of criminal convictions and disciplinary action by other
     regulators, internationally.

These developments, essential if registration is to be based upon
a public – i.e. essentially pupil based – view of registration, and to
safeguard the system of registration more widely in terms of
international movement and 'suitability', are likely to form the
agenda for the development of registration and regulation over the
next few years. Whether registration will apply as a compulsory
requirement to those teachers in sectors where it is not currently a
requirement – particularly the independent school sector – is a matter
for longer-term consideration, bearing in mind that regulation
of child safety and welfare through the DfES is already part of the
system.

Chapter 6

Be prepared

Kate Myers

> There are two kinds of beach front homeowners on the south shore of Long Island: those who have faced serious erosion, and those who will. Similarly, there are two kinds of schools: those that have faced a serious crisis situation, and those that will.
>
> (Lerner 1997, quoted in Lerner *et al.* p. 96)

It has become both a cliche and an understatement to say that we are living in uncertain times and school leaders (like leaders elsewhere) must operate in this context. With regard to the issues raised in this book, they have to make decisions within a context of changing and changeable public perceptions. Clearly, our sexuality is part of our identity. Far less clear is how much of our sexual identity it is proper to reveal to our line managers, our colleagues and our charges.

Many would argue that individual sexual preferences in themselves are not of any concern to 'the authorities'. It is only when the behaviour arising from these actions impacts on the institution that they become the business of the head. However, the same actions can be perceived very differently depending on the sexuality and circumstances of those concerned.

Attitudes towards what is considered 'proper' are different in different communities and they change over time, posing an ongoing dilemma for school leaders. When dealing with these issues, headteachers have to consider that attitudinal change, although widespread, does not necessarily mean there is a consensus, particularly amongst the stakeholders of their particular school. As well as considering their own personal beliefs and values, headteachers have to draw on the schools' contextual and strategic intelligences to read and understand the values of the community within which they are operating and make an ethical decision based on the information gained (MacGilchrist, Myers and Reed, 1997). Making decisions about these issues may be easier in a community where values and goals are shared (assuming the head subscribes to these values). When this is not the case the difficulties can be increased.

Dealing with allegations of abuse

Although this book is mainly about dealing with sexual behaviour relating to adults and young people over the age of 16 it is worth remembering here that school leaders also have to be prepared to deal with allegations of abuse from staff to younger pupils. Dealing with these situations can be a lonely and devastating experience.

Once reported, the staff involved are forbidden to discuss the case with anyone, even their immediate family. There are enormous and often conflicting pressures dealing with allegations of abuse and these pressures can continue for a long period of time waiting for a court case to be scheduled and then through the trial. The consequences of dealing with extremely sensitive issues and not being able to unwind or 'download' with family or friends by discussing the daily occurrences can have enormous impact, even on the most resilient leaders. The understandable rule of silence also means that colleagues who are not directly involved are unlikely to know the 'whole truth'. Innuendo and gossip abound and leaders are power-less to put the facts (as they see them) into the arena. Allegiances and divisions occur that would probably not if the facts were known. The leaders may be seen as being unnecessarily hard on a 'good teacher' and have little support in the school. Much of their time will be taken up dealing with the case rather than running the school. As one head put it 'It takes over your life and consumes all your energy. It's like being in a cocoon, deprived of reality.' The impact on the school and its community can be significant.

The following is a joint statement from a headteacher and chair of governors of a large primary school. The chair of governors was a parent governor and a teacher at another school. The school serves a small town, where 'everyone knows everyone', hence some particular difficulties the head and chair faced when a parent made the first complaint against a respected male deputy head.

They have asked to remain anonymous. Six years on, the enormous personal cost to these leaders from dealing with this case is still evident. This is how they noted their story.

What happened?

The deputy head was dismissed following a governors' investigation into allegations of inappropriate touching of pupils over a period of time. The teacher took a grievance against the dismissal. It took over two years before the case was finally resolved, the day before it was due to be heard in court. The teacher concerned moved from the district to another education authority and is now teaching in a rural area.

The context

Small town syndrome. The families knew each other well. For example, the chair of governor's son was a friend of the deputy head's son. Many staff were friendly with the deputy's immediate or extended family.

Impact on the school

- Division and polarisation of staff
- Shifting many of head's responsibilities to acting deputy in order to free up time for head to deal with the case
- Actual cost to the school for some of the legal advice
- No-win situation
- Not able to answer staff queries because of 'confidentiality of case'
- Tension, rumour and innuendo amongst staff
- Impact on the community – rumour and uncertainty, needing reassurance that the school was OK
- Concern over future impact of school if the teacher had returned to the school. Would vast numbers take their children from the school?
- Testing of governors' solidarity – collective intelligence of governors a plus
- The lingering effect of the situation within the school's culture

Support

We were members of a national governors association and therefore able to access advice and guidance from them. They gave helpful support, e.g. industrial advice on employment. They were excellent.

- Verbal and practical support of other local heads; 'there but for the grace of God . . . '
- Offers of sharing the load for some school tasks

Aloneness

- Lack of external, official involvement. The governors were the employers and that was that!
- Accusatory attitude of the teachers' union towards the governors
- Feelings of uncertainty and vulnerability.

Impact on own job

- Time commitment huge!
- Personal energy input huge
- The two-year length of the situation. Will it ever end?
- That the head and chair of governors were teachers also, and members of the teachers' union we were up against
- Frustration at the impact on the school's culture
- Speculation on impact of this on our own future careers, due to small size of community and isolation
- At times an almost total inability to work effectively.

Impact on home life

- Stress brought home
- Inability to discuss with partners
- Abusive phone calls
- Lack of sleep

- Occasional and unavoidable contact outside of school with supporters of the teacher, e.g. meeting particular shop assistants when undertaking routine shopping.

Personal learning

- Professional development you didn't need, but learnt much from!
- Experience of going through a criminal trial
- The interaction between education and the law
- The constraints of the law
- Sometimes conflicting legal advice from different advisers
- Collective intelligence of the governors, a plus.

Would we do it again?

- Now nervous of any situation in school which could result in industrial action. (We know what we could be in for!)
- Disappointment at the official body responsible for teacher registration at re-registering him and allowing him to continue teaching
- Still comes back to haunt us. At times reference made to the case in social or work situations. Judgements still passed on us and we can't say a thing.
- One of the hardest things was having to write a reference for him as part of the settlement. The morality of this we still find hard to cope with.

Advice to others

- Seek advice *from the beginning*
- Don't do *anything* without seeking advice
- Know who your friends are, but remember they always talk!
- Refer to school policies and procedures. (Always keep key policies and procedures up to date).

- Work as a subcommittee, *never one person*. Information sharing between subcommittees is critical.
- Mutual support of subcommittee
- Keep rest of governors informed continually, otherwise the rumour machine hits them.
- Document everything; telephone calls, conversations, etc. even when it doesn't seem important.
- But remember that everything you write down can be viewed by others at some stage!
- Legal exchange of data before trial
- Don't discuss with family, friends, colleagues; they always talk!
- Be prepared for the rumour machine to work overtime!!!
- Be prepared for high levels of personal stress
- Be prepared for inability at times to do your own job.
- Be prepared for the issue to go home with you. Can't leave it at work.
- The importance of maintaining your composure, especially publicly.
- Ensure as much as possible that the purpose of the school continues uninterrupted.
- Be wary of any potential media involvement. *No statements* except via advisers.
- Be prepared for a high personal cost.
- Be prepared to compromise your values.

Concluding comments

We did what we did because we 100% believed what happened and knew morally this had to be addressed. We addressed it as a board of governors, by dismissing him as the right thing to do, in order to protect the children WE had a duty of care for. We were not able to protect future children he may teach, which was hard to accept. Will the same thing happen again? Only time will tell. Would WE do it all over again???

(Anonymous submission)

The question hanging at the end of their statement is a reminder of the personal cost that can be the consequence of dealing with such issues. Heads have to be mindful of publicity (and its consequences) as well as what is best for the individuals concerned and the school – now and in the future. Leading a school in a time of uncertainty is a complex proposition and one fraught with risks.

The way heads react to changed attitudes to sexuality and how they interpret these changes in their school is open to scrutiny and in some cases legal action. School leaders need to be confident and equipped to deal with these issues as and when they arise. So how could they be prepared?

Prevention is better than cure . . .

Schools in the UK and elsewhere have emergency procedures for fire and other potential risks, such as bomb attacks, floods and accidents. In order to put these procedures in place, the school as an institution anticipates what might happen and plans its reactions in order to ensure the safety of everyone concerned. In well run schools the procedures will be practised and the policy will be revised and updated on a regular basis. Everyone should know what to do in the case of such an emergency.

Many schools are now developing similar procedures for other potential critical incidents. Critical incidents might include those related to the theme of this book as well as murder (of pupil or member of staff), bereavement, chronic illness, mental illness, serious criminal behaviour, and other issues which can affect staff, students and parents. One way of being prepared is to have clear guidelines about what is and what is not appropriate behaviour. This is more clear-cut with regard to pupil–teacher relations but less so when dealing with relationships between staff and between staff and other adults connected with the school. Whichever category, it is useful to have plans ready for dealing with the press in case sensitive situations reach the public arena.

> Lurid headlines can cause lasting damage to a school's repu-
> tation, and some headteachers and governors respond to
> unwelcome media interest by 'battening down the hatches' and
> refusing to speak to reporters. However, this approach will not
> make the problem go away and could be counter-productive. If
> the headteacher or chair of governors will not talk to journalists,

other people almost certainly will, often anonymously. Any school in this position would therefore be well advised to give its own side of the story by issuing a straightforward, factual statement.

(Cooper and Curtis, 2000, p. 42)

Schools can obtain advice on these matters from either their local authority press office or media relations firms.

Relationships between adults in the school

Until very recently, social customs and conventions have not made it easy to discuss sexuality issues in 'polite society'. This has meant that dealing with these issues in an open way, and with integrity, has often been quite difficult. Assuming the climate has changed somewhat, school leaders could take advantage of these changing attitudes. They could introduce these topics as items of discussion with staff and governors.

Potential problem analysis (PPA) could be utilised here (Freedman, 2001). Discussing how leaders in the business world need to prepare for the aftermath of the destruction of the Twin Towers in New York, Freedman, President of worldwide strategy at an international management consultancy (2001) wrote:

> Leaders now realise that an asymmetric assault can come at any time, in any place and from anywhere. Accordingly, they need to dedicate a larger portion of their resources to identifying such potential problems and making plans to deal with them . . . We call the process of identifying future problems and planning both preventive and contingent action potential problem analysis (PPA). In these uncertain times, government officials and senior executives need to ask the PPA questions in a thorough and creative manner.
>
> (p. 9)

Though the critical incidents discussed in this book are not the same as those envisaged by Freedman, PPA could be helpful to school leaders addressing critical incidents. School leaders could undertake the exercise on their own, with the senior team or a wider group of staff members. In this context PPA would focus on discussions about how the school community would want to behave in such situations (e.g. what should we do if . . . ?) All the examples cited earlier in the book could be used as scenarios for discussion with questions posed such as: *How would we want to react? What would the consequences be (e.g. for the individuals concerned; the morale [and perhaps morals] of the pupils/teachers/parents/community; the reputation of the school and consequently future enrolment issues)? Who should make the decision? How would we deal with the media?*

(Facilitators would of course have to be sensitive to the possibility that some of the scenarios could currently be being played out between course participants or their colleagues.)

Participants may find it helpful to use an analytical framework that distinguishes the issues. For example, several of the exemplars cited are concerned with 'moral symbolism', that is, the type of role model that should be presented by teachers and heads. This aspect would involve discussion about what sort of role model we want to present and what is expected of us both within school and during out of school hours. A second category includes issues where conflicts of interest could be perceived, for example, favouritism in promotion, performance related pay, etc. Here issues such as *what happens if someone you are having a relationship with is also line-managed by you or you are their line-manager* would be discussed. The third category is about power issues, for example, sexual relations between junior/senior members of the school community ('junior' could mean pupils as well as junior staff). Power is not always as straightforward as it may seem, that is it is not always wielded by the person with the senior status. Nevertheless, there are issues to consider when, for example, a deputy head has a relationship with a young teacher. There may also be issues to consider in this category when teaching staff have relationships with support staff.

Public and press reaction may vary depending on the category. For example, a school might expect to get a different reaction from the media for any stories concerning 'moral symbolism' than those to do with conflicts of interest.

As the scenarios in this book demonstrate, the way most school leaders tackle relationships amongst the adults in the school is on a 'need to know' and individual basis. This may well be the most effective strategy and being discrete will undoubtedly be essential in many cases involving situations between staff. However, guidelines on these issues may also be of use here and help school leaders react in a consistent manner. Using the discussion from the PPA exercise, schools could consider whether there are or should be policies on any or all of three categories discussed. Once policies are established, procedures can be made clear to staff and protocols for disclosing potential conflicts of interest established. Candidates for jobs can be briefed on this as on all other school policies.

At local authority level, groups of senior managers from different schools could meet together to discuss these issues and share experiences. Similar exercises could be included in leadership training programmes. Furthermore, school leaders could find, or be allocated, a 'critical incident buddy'. Buddies would be peers to whom the school leader could turn when they need someone with whom they can try out ideas and discuss issues, before they have to 'go public'.

One possible disadvantage of anticipating and discussing these issues is that constantly talking about potential problems may feed into the 'risk anxiety' culture prevalent currently in the west (Jones, 2001). However, it can also be argued that people used to talking about sexuality and schooling are likely to be less shocked when having to address actual situations. They will also have had practice in considering the issues from a moral and strategic perspective. In this context, practice may not make perfect, but it will almost certainly help.

Relationships between staff and pupils: codes of practice

As suggested above, dealing with staff–pupil relationships is relatively straightforward. Graham Clayton's chapter makes it clear that any sexual relationship (even consensual) between a member of staff and a pupil is potentially a criminal offence. Procedures for dealing with such incidents need to be established and advice included in staff handbooks. In some countries, the teaching profession has developed, or is developing, a code of conduct. (See chapters 5 and 7 for more discussion on this.) Many school authorities and personnel organisations have also developed their own codes. These codes are clear that the way teachers behave in school is very much a professional matter. They are concerned about behaviour directly connected to school business but are not overt about behaviour outside of school hours.

For example, the code published by the Ministry of Education in Ontario, includes all adults involved in the school system:

All participants involved in the publicly funded school system – students, parents or guardians, volunteers, teachers and other staff members – are included in this Code of Conduct whether they are on school property, on school buses or at school-authorized events or activities. Teachers and school staff, under the leadership of their principals, maintain order in the school and are expected to hold everyone to the highest standard of respectful and responsible behaviour. As role models, staff uphold these high standards when they:

- help students work to their full potential and develop their self-worth
- communicate regularly and meaningfully with parents
- maintain consistent standards of behaviour for all students
- demonstrate respect for all students, staff and parents
- prepare students for the full responsibilities of citizenship.
  (Ontario Ministry of Education, 2001)

Some codes have been developed specifically about sexuality issues. These can include detailed advice about physical contact, comforting a pupil in distress, unavoidable contact, private meetings, infatuations and crushes and after school activities. For example, a model code of conduct produced by Cooper and Curtis, 2000, suggests that as 'Teachers . . . are important role models [they] should conduct themselves accordingly'. Their code includes advice about avoiding physical contact and private meetings with pupils, particularly off the premises. It also addresses the issue of 'crushes'.

Infatuations and crushes can involve pupils and staff of both sexes on both a heterosexual and homosexual basis. An employee in such a situation should inform a senior colleague without delay. The situation must be taken seriously and the member of staff should be careful to ensure that no encouragement of any kind is given to the pupil. Careless and insensitive reactions may provoke false accusations. Young, newly qualified teachers must recognise their particular vulnerability to adolescent infatuation.

(Cooper and Curtis, 2000, p. 56)

Emailing and texting messages to students are both relatively new potential problem areas and deserve some discussion amongst staff as to whether they want to devise protocol around these activities too.

According to one author, teachers can help themselves.

> They must record and report if they have any concerns about a child's attitude towards them; if, for instance, the child is being flirtatious or verbally or physically aggressive. They then have evidence of a history of behaviour if an allegation is made later. They should avoid taking children in their cars alone and if a one-to-one conversation with a pupil is needed, colleagues should be aware of this, with the door kept open. Never contact a child outside school without someone knowing.
>
> (Williams, 2004, p. 14)

Cooper and Curtis also suggest that no part of the school premises should be considered anyone's private space – solely for their use.

> Members of staff should not have the opportunity to create private spaces for themselves within the school. Music practice rooms can easily be turned into private places since they are small, sound-proofed and often found in out-of-the-way parts of the school. Other potential danger zones include the care-taker's store cupboards and offices. It is not unusual for the caretaker to be [the] only person with keys to these spaces, as there is usually very little reason for other members of staff to enter them. Similarly technicians' store cupboards or prepa-ration rooms are often tucked away in remote corners of the school that see very little through traffic . . . Managers need to have an overview of how all the accommodation within a school is used and to make sure that no member of staff has sole access to any room or large storage area.
>
> (Cooper and Curtis, 2000, p. 8)

School leaders could work with their colleagues to develop a code that is acceptable and appropriate to their situation. Staff (especially young teachers and teachers in training who may be only a few years older than some of their students) may also find it useful to receive some advice with regard to dealing with pupils who imply or adopt sexual interest from unwanted advances to sexual harassment. Guidance should also include advice about the dangers of socialising with students, particularly in situations where alcohol may be involved. (Cooper and Curtis, 2000). Such guidance could be written and/or delivered in the form of a training session. In order to ensure the messages are memorable the session could include some role play.

As well as individual schools organising their own professional development needs around these issues they could be addressed on leadership courses, union courses, and as an LEA. The final chapter suggests practical ways of doing this.

Chapter 7

Sexing up the flipcharts

Organising professional development on controversial issues

Jim O'Brien

There was once a baron and baroness who lived in a castle surrounded by a moat. There were two ways into the castle. The first was via a drawbridge and the second by small boat, for which a fee was payable to the boatman. One bright morning the baron announced he was going out for the day but before he left he warned his wife, the baroness, in the presence of her servants that if she was not there when he returned, there would be dire consequences. The baroness, bored with little to do around the castle tells her servants to get her ready to go out. She takes no heed of their warnings. She leaves and goes off to the forest where she meets her lover. She forgets the time and it is late when she hurries back to the castle.

Reaching the drawbridge, she discovers the mute gateman is unwilling to let her in; she rushes round to the boatman who demands his usual fee. She doesn't have any money on her. So she seeks out her friend who is anxious to help but reminds her that this is the one day in the year when religion forbids monetary exchanges. The baroness returns to her lover in the woods to seek help but is told in sharp terms that they agreed to have an uncomplicated 'affair' and offers no help. She has little option but to return to the gateman and implore that he let her in. He responds by chopping off her head.

Who is most responsible for the death of the baroness? And what has she got to do with *Teachers Behaving Badly?* But let's begin at the beginning . . .

Using stories is just one of the approaches that are helpful when dealing with sensitive and controversial issues. The storytelling example of the baroness involves several characters and a degree of ambiguity that can generate non-threatening but highly relevant discussion in groups. Having used this particular story on several occasions with groups of teachers including groups of heads, I believe that it is a powerful instigator of debate and thinking which can go on beyond the activity. For example, after one professional development session in which it was told, a participating headteacher wrote:

> There are strong parallels between the position of the gate-keeper in the story and our position as heads (there are many references to heads as gatekeepers in the educational literature). The baron, representing the political ruling classes, uses his power in an arbitrary way to maintain control and stifle societal change and empowerment. Schools, through their headteachers (gatekeepers), offer restricted, highly controlled environments (castles), having little contact with the real world (the forest), in which students (baronesses) are conditioned to accept the rules and the status quo. Teachers (the servant) warn against breaking the rules but ultimately are powerless to restrain the creative enthusiasm of students and their desire to discover the real world instead of the barren, sterile world of the school (castle) in which they spend their days imprisoned.

Of course, it is not simply the story that is important in this particular activity. The associated prioritisation task (see later in the chapter) requires participants to consider, evaluate and clarify their individual and group positions. Invariably, everyone has an opinion. Being challenged to explain what they believe and why, offers participants genuine opportunities for reflective learning and personal development informed by peers. Personal feelings will be revealed, challenged and sometimes modified because of other viewpoints.

If staff are used to continuing professional development (CPD) which tells them the answers, they may be initially disorientated by situations where there are no 'right' answers. Indeed in most of the activities suggested in this chapter there are no clearly defined, well packaged blueprints. Sensitive and controversial issues are often 'messy' and while some people may at an individual level have a fully worked out position (this is rarely the case) the key to development of individuals and the school community is the creation of opportunities where teachers are able to reflect on their positions in a 'safe' environment and take responsibility for their own learning. Stories, and other activities described later, can help to achieve this.

This chapter focuses on professional development principles and suggests approaches for the design and delivery of effective professional development activities specifically for such situations. Cases cited in previous chapters are used as a context, prompt or illustration for CPD. The suggestions and exemplar activities in this chapter can be customised so that schools or groups of staff (e.g. heads, LEA advisers, union learning representatives, education consultants) and providers of CPD, can make them appropriate to their own needs and contexts.

The testimony from the head and chair of governors discussed in chapter 6, demonstrates the potential impact on people, institutions and the community when critical incidents arise and the need of organisations to be prepared to deal with these cases. Potential problem analysis (PPA) was suggested as an approach that would allow discussions with staff and governors and other stakeholders. PPA used in this way can provide learning opportunities and be an effective form of CPD.

Teacher CPD traditionally, has a number of purposes, e.g. to introduce teachers to new methodologies; to update or adapt their practice; to provide information about new curricula or policies or to prepare them for specific initiatives, e.g. numeracy and literacy strategies. Other vital aspects of CPD are to allow teachers to reflect on their experience; to promote debate and dialogue about issues of interest or concern; to avoid knee-jerk reactions and to encourage consistency of behaviour amongst colleagues. All these are more likely to happen in schools where values are overt and shared and where learning about these issues is seen as ongoing.

Critical or controversial incidents, such as those described throughout this book, can be used as a basis for the design of a number of CPD activities that may assist in the promotion of a learning community. Such a community is one that sees the need to clarify its own organisational value base *in order* to develop policy and key procedures. In these schools, a climate of co-operation, trust and respect exists and sensitive issues are not ignored. Appropriate teacher development, even in difficult areas, is encouraged and staff are prepared collectively and individually to face difficult circumstances as they arise.

Dealing with values in CPD

There are at least two distinct ideological approaches to CPD – training and education. Each has a different purpose and ethos although the boundaries are not always as clear-cut as they may seem at first glance as values permeate both approaches. Training is normally dominated by competences and standards, underpinned by a desire for teachers to conform and to perform at specific levels. The education aspect of CPD stresses the professional autonomy and critical reflectiveness of teachers, suggesting that they are able to select appropriate behaviours and to be able to justify them when necessary.

McGettrick suggests that in a society with a plurality of values it is necessary to pay attention to self-esteem and the 'inner-self' of the teacher through staff development:

> This goes beyond a concern for technical or pedagogical competence, and encompasses support for the needs of the teacher as a person. The teacher is a person who needs to be valued, to be given dignity in life as well as in the profession of teaching.
>
> (1994, p. 117)

Issues of sexuality can generate polarised viewpoints, where values are very much to the fore and such values need to be shared, articulated and understood by CPD providers and recipients alike. CPD that encourages exploration of values is very different from CPD providing training on some new piece of software or updating computer skills. However, much training is also underpinned by values. For example, training on literacy is very far from being value free. There are clear connections here with fundamental values and beliefs about pedagogy and teaching and learning. Unfortunately issues of values and opportunities for critique are not often addressed when training is the dominant approach. However, with the Code of Professional Values and Practice for Teachers (General Teacher Council, England, 2002) CPD will have to relate to value issues more and we need to be prepared to offer appropriately thought-through opportunities. The code adopted by GTC England and discussed in greater detail by David James in chapter 5:

> recognises that teachers work within a framework of legislation with many lines of accountability. The complicated and varied

roles that teachers need to fulfil make teaching one of the most demanding and rewarding professions . . . teachers work within a framework of equal opportunities and other relevant legislation, statutory guidance and school policies. Within this framework, teachers challenge stereotypes and oppose prejudice to safeguard equality of opportunity, respecting individuals regardless of gender, marital status, religion, colour, race, ethnicity, class, sexual orientation, disability and age . . .

Teachers support their colleagues in achieving the highest professional standards. They are fully committed to sharing their own expertise and insights in the interests of the people they teach and are always open to learning from the effective practice of their colleagues. Teachers respect the rights of other people to equal opportunities and to dignity at work. They respect confidentiality where appropriate . . . Teachers support the place of the school in the community and appreciate the importance of their own professional status in society. They recognise that professionalism involves using judgement over appropriate standards of personal behaviour.

(Code of Professional Values and Practice for
Teachers, GTCE, 2002)

The Standard for Chartered Teacher in Scotland (SEED, 2002) lists *values and personal commitments* first in its four key and interdependent components. The other components are *professional knowledge and understanding*; *professional and personal attributes*; and *professional action*. Four central professional values and personal commitments are proffered:

- effectiveness in promoting learning in the classroom;
- critical self-evaluation and development;
- collaboration and influence;
- educational and social values.

The standard offers illustrations of core educational and social values, such as concern for truth, personal responsibility, equality, social justice and inclusion. A chartered teacher might exemplify such values by:

- evaluating his or her teaching and pupils' learning in relation to pupils' personal, social, moral and cultural development

- assessing how the school culture and practices promote, or could promote more effectively, citizenship, personal responsibility, social competence, social justice and life in a multi-ethnic society
- working to enhance pupils' development and their understanding of social values in a pluralist society.

(Standard for Chartered Teacher, SEED, 2002)

Programmes of CPD which lead to chartered teacher status must recognise the importance of work-based learning and experience and teacher professional action must evince a concern for moral and ethical values. There is an emphasis on values too in the preparation of Scottish heads who are expected to:

- hold, articulate and argue for professionally defensible educational values
- [be] able to articulate and exemplify a moral and ethical perspective in relation to their own and the school's practice and organisation.

(Standard for Headship, SOEID, 1998)

CPD programmes which meet the requirements of both the above standards are professionally accredited (by GTC Scotland) and validated as post-graduate awards by universities in partnership with other CPD providers and teacher employers. Such programmes are long-term in their nature, equivalent to at least a year's full-time learning and development on the part of participants, and assessment requirements demand discernible impact on schools and classrooms through evidence of work-based learning.

Not all staff though have the opportunity or the resilience to participate in long-term accredited courses where these issues can be discussed over time and in depth. Short courses for peer groups or interventions at school level have their place too. Glover and Law stress the need for staff to engage in discussion about values held:

A lack of shared values is likely to hinder developments in any organization, particularly where staff regard change as a threat to their established roles, practices or attitudes.

(1996, p. 149)

Glover and Law regard one-off courses as important in raising awareness and providing the impetus for more substantial CPD work, especially when considering personal and professional values. There is some evidence that one-off CPD courses or interventions have little impact on teachers perhaps because the activities are not concrete or immediate enough for their circumstances or there is little or no follow-up. However, at institutional level when they involve the whole staff body, one-off courses can offer opportunities for the promotion of shared understanding and influence on decision making. And outside of school at peer group level, e.g. groups of heads or deputies, such courses can offer opportunities for net-working and establishing peer support systems.

Identifying specific values

What values might be important for teacher interaction and help to promote effective CPD? Smith (1997, pp. 42–3) discusses the value of respect, which, if evident in professional life will be accompanied by several other values such as *openness*, *integrity*, and *fairness*. She cites earlier work by Watson and Ashton (1995), who suggest that *openness* in this context has four components:

- openness to fresh evidence;
- openness to the experience of others;
- openness to appreciating the needs and situations of others;
- openness to critical assessment especially about self-delusion.

Integrity is concerned with honesty and the 'vigorous use of our critical faculties in order to develop a sounder understanding of our beliefs and a commitment to principled behaviour'. *Fairness*, Smith suggests, 'relates to a sense of justice, equity and consideration for the rights of others'.

These values are important if professional development is generally to be meaningful and particularly so in relation to the themes discussed in earlier chapters. Such themes may be controversial for participants or they may wish to avoid consideration of them. Certainly many of these areas will touch personally on many colleagues and the values that they hold. It is important to provide opportunities for professional development and reflection on these particular areas because the themes discussed throughout are or will be issues which schools and their staff increasingly will have to relate to.

In recent years there has been an increasing interest in values education in the curriculum but Stephenson, Ling, Burman and Cooper (eds) indicate that teacher respondents in their research:

> In many cases . . . were unable to reflect critically on and to articulate their attitude to values and values education. In some cases it appeared that they had avoided, consciously or unconsciously, the sources of many of their basic assumptions regarding values.
>
> (1998, p. 168)

This would suggest that much needs to be done in this area and CPD opportunities for serving teachers may increasingly have to include value issues in their design and makeup.

Designing CPD activities

The examples cited in this book can be used as a development resource for designing a range of CPD opportunities e.g. school, cluster, LEA, union based or for leadership courses.

The CPD activities that follow, recognise that short CPD activities of around two hours, half a day or a whole day can provide opportunities which will develop shared understanding and influence on decision making at institutional level and lead possibly to more sustained reflection on these important themes. Each of these sessions demonstrates how the elements of the materials in earlier chapters might be used for professional development activities in addition to the way they are discussed in this book. The emphasis here is deliberately on workshops or courses or activities, for groups of staff. However, many of the activities could be used by task or working groups to encourage initial consideration of the themes or to clarify reactions. Timing for particular elements within activities are offered as guidelines. Guidance is provided on creating or designing professional development activities. I am not necessarily suggesting experiential learning here – particularly when we are dealing with matters relating to sexual behaviour! I do stress, however, the notion of 'activities' because, in my experience, active involvement by staff in the form of sharing viewpoints, problem solving or collaborative decision making (through discussions in small groups for example) is critical if CPD on any topic is to be effective.

Adult learning theories suggest a number of important considerations for the planning, design and teaching processes involved in CPD:

- Short bursts of learning, with materials broken up into small manageable units.
- Start with concrete issues relevant to the present needs of the teachers – this may not follow a logical sequence; where possible assist by using their own examples and experiences.
- Engage directly in the theme; learning by doing the task.
- Don't tell or do it for them – engage the participants so that learning is active and involved.
- Move from specific issues to general principles, illustrated by concrete examples. While a lecture or direct teaching can be a highly effective means of transmitting information, most lectures are less effective in the promotion of thought. Attitude shift is more difficult when recipients are passive.

School based CPD

When engaging with sensitive issues, the question of climate is critical. Schools which routinely involve themselves in meaningful self-evaluation strategies (MacBeath, 1999) will have a climate of trust and openness. Professional development co-ordinators (PDCs), through day-to-day engagement, will have knowledge about individuals and groups of colleagues. The PDC's sensitivity to relationships and context will play an important role in establishing an open climate – one in which the ground rules for dialogue and engagement are worked out collectively in advance, are made explicit and where colleagues know the limits of confidentiality. A possible strategy is to consult on such ground rules through the school's CDP committee where one exists. A draft process might be obtained from an experienced external facilitator and discussed and modified as necessary. The external facilitator might work with a staff group to consider the limits of interaction acceptable within the context.

Such preparation is important. The controversial themes of this book will mean that colleagues may have firm views or principles (considered and informed or ill-informed to some degree or another), or alternatively they may have avoided formulating a personal position perhaps in the hope that circumstances will never challenge them on particular issues. If they are being 'talked at' about values then questions such as 'whose values are these?' or 'where are these values coming from?' might arise. Such questioning if pursued by groups would be useful if they were afforded enough time for critical reflection and discussion but, while teacher-centred methods are legitimate, adult learning theory suggests that teaching methods where the teacher adopts a more facilitative role rather than direct teaching can be more appropriate. The tutor or PDC is responsible for providing the learning situation but cannot control the outcomes.

A list of possible methods might include brainstorming; buzz groups; debate; discussion groups; interviews; snowballing; role-play, simulation and games. Other methods that can be added to the list include storytelling exemplified by the baroness story at the beginning of this chapter; consensus exercises; in-tray exercises; critical incident technique; rapid information exchange; nominal group technique; and prioritisation exercises in addition to study groups and working parties. Many of these techniques are discussed by MacBeath (1988, pp. 80–101).

Principles of teacher professional development

Needs analysis

It is generally accepted that effective professional development is based on a needs analysis so that whatever is offered or designed reflects the needs of participants. As noted, long-term planned CPD may have more lasting and profound effect but there will be occasions when particular issues arise which could benefit from some spontaneous CPD.

The school development plan (SDP) will often identify high level needs but some more work may be required when developing specific CPD activities. There are essentially three types of need evident in schools:

- *Individual needs*: These will involve developing skills and knowledge to teach more effectively.
- *Team needs*: Developing common understandings, expertise and approaches for departmental or pastoral teams, stage teams, or senior management teams.
- *Whole-school needs*.

Establishing common values, developing and implementing policy

Some of this book's themes will relate to the establishment of common values among similarly placed professionals, in teams and at whole school level, but there are associated issues with policy and individual actions and behaviours.

Many schools have CPD committees charged with aiding the PDC in the identification of needs and in arranging how best they might be met. Colleagues can often provide insights, and other experiences, plus case studies for possible use. They may know what is happening in other LEAs or schools, or perhaps might be studying for another qualification and can provide the names of 'experts' in related areas.

It is always important to know where you are as an organisation when you embark on planning and providing CPD opportunities. What is the current situation or expectations around sensitive issues in your school? Heads, or professional development co-ordinators, when considering professional development needs in this area might want to consider some of the following questions. The meetings in themselves may prove to be learning opportunities. The answers you obtain may suggest whether you need to consider if there is a need for CPD and how you might address such a need:

- Are staff clear about the behavioural norms (including dress code) expected within the school and in their outside school activities? Should this be an issue for frank discussion or development of a clear policy statement within the school?
- What would the school's reaction be to the scenario highlighted at the beginning of this book? Do you think the headteacher responded in an appropriate way? Would you do the same or react differently? Why?
- Should there be a code about 'conflict of interest' for example if a head of department is having a relationship with someone in their department?
- Are there additional concerns in faith schools in relation to sensitive issues such as those discussed in earlier chapters? Who might best advise about such concerns?
- Can there be a divide between the private and the public in relation to such sensitive issues?
- Does an effective policy about sexual harassment exist and do staff adhere to it?

Of course you may meet resistance from different members of your staff when establishing controversial topics as a necessary theme for professional development. What if parents were to find out what staff were discussing, would it affect recruitment? Would parents and the extended local community be shocked or outraged? Is it preferable to hope that nothing ever occurs? Do schools have a duty to educate their community as much as their pupils?

As noted in chapter 1, no head wants to court scandal or bad publicity, so why would you generate it by preparing for such issues? One answer may be so that if a situation should arise it can be dealt with openly, honestly and with concern for the individuals caught up in any incident. A balance has always to be struck when meeting individual, team or corporate needs and additionally prioritising of needs is deemed essential. If you were considering the need to prepare your staff in relation to some of the issues discussed in this book, which of the issues you have read about in earlier chapters might require attention in your school? How much of a priority is this and how do you know? Have there been local incidents where your reaction has been 'There but for the grace of God . . . '

If you bring an external provider into school, how assured are you that they will deal with the topic/theme appropriately? An advantage of an external provider in such a situation is that they may be neutral but a downside will be that they may remain unaware of the nuances being played out amongst the staff. The role of the PDC is critical in providing an informed brief to the external provider who should shape provision based on the brief, knowing critically where staff are at in relation to a theme and developing appropriate learning opportunities.

How appropriate would it be to establish a small working group on drawing up a policy and set of procedures on dealing with a situation of a salacious sex story emerging from your school? Would this be only the start of a more sustained period of reflection and development at personal, team and school level and how would you hope to use such a working group as a catalyst for further staff development?

External courses

External conferences and courses may prove less threatening to staff when considering controversial issues. Staff who attend these can remain relatively anonymous, especially in a large group.

Relationships, past and current, within the group are also less likely to exist, whereas within a large school staff it is always likely that there will be participants who are engaged in such a relationship or who are aware of other members of the group who are in this situation. Does the LEA or other providers of CPD offer courses or provision in these areas and what are the cost implications? Who amongst the staff would it be appropriate to send? If no such opportunities exist can you organise some through for example, the LEA, one of the teacher/headteacher unions, or with a cluster of local schools? What sort of feedback and follow-up would be useful to the school?

Sample professional development activities: teachers behaving badly?

The sample CPD activities that follow are designed to introduce and to cover controversial issues in a non-threatening and often indirect impersonal way. Even if participants have direct experience of some of the issues being considered as in the 'Teachers as role models?' exercise, the fact that the issues are depersonalised and on cards compels engagement. People can stand back a bit from a particular issue even if it is a direct concern to them. However, PDCs may have to be careful when using the scenario activity as it could illustrate a real ongoing issue within a school which staff might recognise. In such circumstances another scenario should be substituted or developed. The scenarios used are taken from earlier chapters, but the national and local press and media routinely deal with similar 'factual' issues and examples, even if they are often sensationalised and reflect hypocritical attitudes. You might wish staff colleagues to provide examples and illustrations using a non-judgemental brain-storming technique, but be wary and alert to possible difficulties this may lead to. On occasions people can use such sessions to disclose information about themselves. A PDC or facilitator will have to treat this with great sensitivity. Sometimes, people are inadvertently prompted to disclose personal information. For example, in early training for teachers on child protection issues, some facilitators suggested that statistically there would be x per cent of people sitting there who had suffered one form of abuse or another in their child-hood and this at times led to disclosure. The skilled facilitator will be able to deal with inappropriate disclosure or will apply the estab-lished ground rules, discussed above, to deal with such a situation.

Colleagues should be engaged at the design stage whenever possible so that their needs can be built into a programme of activities for CPD. This will promote a sense of ownership of the theme or topic and such CPD may become viewed as more worthwhile. If a series of sessions is planned, such dialogue will take account of the balance and sequence of activities envisaged. Where groups of staff are concerned needs will vary, but the engagement of staff with each other can often be a powerful learning experience. This may encourage staff to feel confident, respected and valued and they should be given opportunities to reflect, individually and in groups, on materials/stimuli presented during CPD sessions; this would avoid reliance on 'stand and deliver' approaches.

Activities

Activity 1: clarifying our values

A 1–2 hour session based on a storytelling technique (using the baron and baroness story described at the beginning of the chapter)

Purpose

- to promote discussion on a range of interpersonal issues;
- to consider principles of effective intervention;
- to identify practices which exemplify those principles.

Process

1 Tutor/facilitator tells a story (10 minutes).

Tell the story of the baron and the baroness which you will find at the beginning of this chapter.
  Put the seven characters on a flipchart or acetate

  Baron, baroness, gateman, servant(s), lover, friend, boatman.

Ask the group:

  Who is most responsible for the death of the baroness?

1 Do not offer any further comment on the story or answer any questions about it.

2   Participants consider and record their response individually (5 minutes).
3   Then divide into small groups (30 minutes).

Explain the rules for the group activity:

(a) Listen to other people's point of view, do not simply argue your own position.
(b) Make sure everyone has a chance to share their view.
(c) No voting or averaging allowed reaching the group decision, participants should weigh up the strongest arguments.

The group share their individual prioritisations and their task is to reach an agreement about the order of responsibility for the death of the baroness.

   Ask groups in turn to share their order and to justify it (20–30 minutes).

5   The facilitator should record on the flipchart and clarify the group's assumptions, challenge their interpretations and reasons for decisions.

6   Some questions for the facilitator to pose:

•   What do you think of the characters in this story?
•   What moral issues are posed by this story?
•   Is the boatman too mean or entrepreneurial?
•   Has the baron been arbitrary in his warning of dire consequences, what might the legal position be?
•   Who had the easiest options to help the baroness?
•   Who risked the most if they helped her?
•   Is gender an issue? What if the lover was a woman?

What if a different version of the story involved:

   a head, deputy, caretaker, school secretary, a pupil, chair of governors, teacher and was concerned with a controversial or critical incident around a liaison in the school between the deputy and a pupil?

Activity 2: dealing with sensitive matters

A 2 × 1–2 hour session using scenarios to prompt discussion in groups.

Purpose

- to review particular scenarios that schools may have to deal with using real examples.
- to highlight policy issues and necessary actions.

Process

A

1   Prepare in advance cards with the scenarios. Each group consider the following cases/scenarios:

Scenario 1

A student teacher is having considerable discipline problems and is in danger of failing her course. She complains to her tutor that the head of department (one of the best teachers in the school) is sexually harassing her. It so happens that the head of department is married to one of the deputies.

What could be done? What do you do? What are the consequences?

Scenario 2

You knock on the deputy's door about an hour after school has finished. You find the deputy and the school secretary both half dressed and in a compromising situation.

What could you do? What do you do? What are the consequences?

(Does the sex of the deputy/secretary make a difference? Does it make a difference if the staff involved are the same sex?).

Scenario 3

A parent tells you she is not going to let her son be taught PE by Mr P. because she knows he is 'queer' and she doesn't want him anywhere near her child. What's more she doesn't think he should be in the school at all and is planning to tell everyone she can find.

What could you do? What do you do? What are the consequences?

Scenario 4

A governor tells you that Mr J,. a young teacher in the school, attended a party in the neighbourhood on Saturday where several pupils were present. He suggests that Mr J.'s behaviour left a lot to be desired.

What could you do? What do you do? What are the consequences?

Scenario 5

You are slowly becoming aware that two teachers in the school are probably having an affair. They are both married and parents. You are not sure whether this is common knowledge in the staffroom or whether it is any business of yours.

What could you do? What do you do? What are the consequences?

(Does it make a difference if they are the same sex?)

2   Issue the cards and request that groups choose two of the scenarios (or alternatively issue specific scenarios to each group). The groups should consider the issues the scenarios raise and generate a group response to the questions posed.

3   Have groups report back and discuss the general and specific points raised

4 When does the private become professional? Prepare an OHT or equivalent with the questions Felicity Haynes poses in chapter 1. (You may find it useful to re-read chapter 1 before the session):

(a) What are the consequences, both short and long term, for me and others, and do the benefits of any possible action outweigh the harmful effects?

(b) Are all the agents in this situation being consistent with their own past actions and beliefs? That is, are they acting according to an ethical principle/ethical principles that they would be willing to apply in any other similar situation? Are they doing to others as they would they would do unto them?

(c) Are they responding to the needs of others as human beings? Do they care about other people in this situation as persons with feelings like themselves?

(Haynes, 1998, pp. 28–9)

Discuss these questions in relation to the scenarios.

B REVISIT THE SCENARIOS IN CHAPTER 2

For each scenario ask the group:

(a) How would they react in this situation?
(b) What would the consequences be for each different reaction?

Activity 3: teachers as role models?

A 1–2 hour session using a card sort activity.

Purpose

- to consider the notion of sensitive issues;
- to encourage clarification of views, values and share reactions to specific statements. (The statements are derived from chapters 2 and 3.)

Process

1 Prepare the following statements on a set of cards and create a set for each group.

2 Encourage groups to reflect and share their views on each statement.

3 Then *prioritise* 1–9 as follows, by sticking the cards on a flipchart in the following pattern.

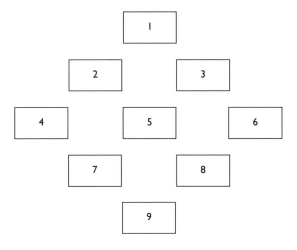

In their day to day behaviour teachers should reflect the traditional and pervading mores of society

Teachers should accept obscene phone calls, comments about their bodies, sex lives and obscene gestures as part of the job

Flirting with fellow staff and pupils is just innocent fun

Teachers have no private time – being a professional involves a responsibility to behave appropriately at all times

Sexual banter is harmless

Drugs, and alcohol misuse outside of school should always be subject to disciplinary action

There is too much moral panic about children and their vulnerability in the world outside their home

Sexuality is often used as a controlling device in schools

Teachers are rightly expected to be role models for their students

Direct action works in situations of sexual harassment

Certain forms of masculinity are OK as a means of controlling boys

It is risky to ignore complaints of sexual misconduct

'Abnormal' behaviour should be treated sympathetically, e.g. a member of staff undergoing a sex change

Pupil culture often reflects the models of behaviour offered by staff

Innuendo can be embarrassing for many and sexual harassment for some

There needs to be a dress code for teachers

Homophobic abuse by colleagues, parents or pupils should not be tolerated

Whatever the circumstances, sexual relations between teachers and pupils are immoral

It is different if women teachers become sexually involved with pupils

Relationships based on love between staff and pupils should be treated differently from abusive ones

Too many young women students are overt in their sexuality and constantly use it to bait teachers

Activity 4: sensitive issues and the law

A 1–2 hour session using a study group approach.

Purpose

To familiarise oneself with some of the legal aspects pertaining to sensitive issues.

Process

1   Obtain copies of the Sexual Offences Act 2003 for group members, and request that they read chapter 4 of this book, particularly the section entitled 'Teachers are special'

2   Consider the following questions as a group:

What are the main differences introduced by the Sexual Offences Act 2003?

Why is the Act particularly concerned with the protection of children?

How is downloading child pornography dealt with and what can be the consequences?

How does the Act impinge on activities in schools?

Are teachers special enough to be treated differently from other members of society?

Activity 5: developing policy and procedures

A 1–2 hour session using a working group approach.

Purpose

To consider some advice and to reflect on policy required

Process

Working group members should familiarise themselves with chapter 5

1 Obtain copies of the local authority's code of conduct for the group

2 Ask the group the following questions:

- How does the code help us in this school?
- Do we need anything clarified or expanded?
- If so, who will do that?
- Is there a case to develop a school code based on the local authority version?

3 Get the group to consider possible action by heads and the school when faced with misconduct or a controversial issue. Read the section titled 'Initial assessment' in chapter 5. Ask the group:

- What do you think of the advice offered here?
- What would help the head and staff to form an initial assessment of the presenting issue?
- When should schools seek additional help?
- What agencies are likely to be able to offer help?
- What is the case for informal advice rather than disciplinary action being considered?

The sample activities above serve as illustrations of possible uses of the content and discussion around the themes and topics considered in earlier chapters. You might use them in full, but careful review in the light of needs analysis within your own setting may encourage amendment or customisation.

Conclusion

Social behaviours, morality and controversial issues can never be removed from education and schooling. Schools have to mirror a changing society struggling with the pace of technological innovation and globalisation. Traditional values are inevitably challenged and found to be out of step with prevailing ideas and actions. Everyday life no longer has a series of moral or ethical certainties which predetermine behaviour and action in response to difficult circumstances; indeed who is to say what difficult issues or circumstances are?

How prepared are school leaders to deal with sensitive issues and controversial incidents? I have noted that values play an important part in the preparation of prospective Scottish headteachers, but there is little evidence of consideration of sensitive areas as discussed in earlier chapters or the skills of dealing with these being recognised as legitimate content in the related qualification for headship. The National College for School Leadership offers a range of programmes associated with its Framework for Leadership, but such leadership training appears not to include exposure to issues involving sexuality and sexual harassment. As this book has highlighted, many school leaders have no choice but to deal with such concerns.

CPD is recognised by governments, employers and teacher unions as increasingly important for the teaching profession. It helps to update, refresh and prepare teachers for changing circumstances. I have argued here that the controversial and sensitive issues identified and discussed in earlier chapters demand a professional development response. While CPD activities can take many forms, as noted earlier, I would stress the importance of active involvement in working parties or study groups; quality circles; and/or school-based activities/workshops using approaches under-pinning the sample activities above. Such approaches will help to engage groups of heads, prospective leaders at whatever level and/or school staff in worthwhile and increasingly necessary professional development.

Appendix

The following may be useful to colleagues new to organising CPD activities.

Monitoring and evaluation

It is important that each of the CPD activities is monitored and evaluated to determine: whether specific provision has met its purpose – for example a short-term check on the delivery of a school-based session. Often this is done through a short questionnaire, which focuses on items such as: 'Did the activity meet its objectives?' and encourages comment on the content and methodology used. For example:

Please tick as appropriate	Completely	Fairly	To some extent	Hardly	Not at all
I felt the session addressed my needs					
I felt able to express my views					
I became involved in the discussions					
The issues raised were too personal and embarrassing					
The tasks were appropriate					

Analysis of the responses may suggest changes are made in subsequent sessions; for example, a change of presenter, different forms of engaging participants or changes to the tasks. Often the long-term impact it may have on the individual teacher, pupils and school is a neglected aspect, but schools are increasingly conscious of issues associated with 'value for money' and accreditation of experience or gaining credit for achievement. Long-term evaluation of the impact and results of CPD may have to be planned and allowed for in any professional development plan agreed by a school. The same might be said about follow-up to CPD activities.

The activities above are designed to be self-contained as activities but they will often lead to the identification of further development needs or practical action associated with school policy and processes. Staff may wish to talk further about the issues raised and opportunities will have to be found for this. Depending on the climate within your school this might involve small study groups or using local or personal networks to put staff in touch with other colleagues elsewhere. Equally, you might wish to have exemplar material to consider, if developing a statement or policy. There are examples in the previous chapter and many LEAs have such advice readily available on websites. If your own authority does not, others will and such material can now be found readily on professional association or teacher support websites such as NCSL (http://www. ncsl.org.uk) where there is an example of a draft Equal Opportunities school policy.

Practical considerations when delivering CPD

There are some important areas to consider when designing and delivering CPD activity-based sessions, regardless of the focus. Some suggestions are offered but they are neither prescriptive nor exhaustive.

Pre event: organisational details

Make room arrangements including 'breakout space' for smaller groups

- A comfortable environment is always appreciated as are appropriate refreshments
- Organise audio visual requirements and check that they are on-site on the day
- Provide writing materials, pens, flipcharts, sugar paper, drawing pins, 'Blu tack' etc all available
- Do a last minute check!

Pre event: planning, selecting/ customising or designing your activities

Clarify the purpose and the expected outcomes of the session.

- Is it to update colleagues? Or is it to effect some change in the way things are done?
- Are you identifying problems and seeking solutions as a group?
- Are you providing solutions for the group?

If you intend using existing materials or resources are they fit for purpose? For example, does the video available really do the job you want?

Ensure tasks are relevant, engaging, real and meaningful.

- Encourage colleagues to provide you with stimulus materials such as prompts for discussion or case studies
- Is the task clear, will it be straightforward and achievable within the timeframe?
- Will a task generate group trust, enthusiasm and commitment?
- How will a group operate to achieve the task? Is there a need for group leaders? If so, how are they to be selected and briefed?

Plan different combinations of people to suit a particular activity e.g. whole group, smaller groups, pairs or threes and individuals.

Each combination will allow colleagues to feel varying degrees of involvement, to generate many ideas and options, to be active and allow reflection and to develop self-awareness.

- Decide groupings in advance This may avoid colleagues being inhibited and others dominating.

Event: your role

- Set the climate, make colleagues feel relaxed and at ease.
- Be clear about the *purpose* and the outcomes expected of the session.
- Introduce the activities and elements in the session, but be brief. Work out what you will say in advance – use notes sparingly as necessary.
- Engage colleagues, challenging views as necessary – this is not the same as imposing your own viewpoint.
- Encourage participation, challenge dominant behaviour.
- Unobtrusively keep individuals and groups on task.
- If products are required, encourage completion.
- Chair feedback opportunities.
- Don't impose your own views and opinions.
  - Confirm everyone agrees with what is being recorded e.g. on flipchart or have a group scribe or 'post-its';
  - Seek explanations and clarifications where necessary
- Ensure the session runs to time.

Post event: recommended actions

- Collate and analyse the evaluation forms.
- Collate and process feedback responses from tasks and activities and issue to all participants.
- Review and reflect on your own role.

References

Abrams, F. (2003) How are we doing?, *Times Educational Supplement*, 21 November, pp. 8–10

Adler, S. (2000) 'When Ms Muffet fought back: a view of work on children's books since the 1970s', in K. Myers (ed.) *Whatever Happened to Equal Opportunities in Schools: Gender Equality Initiatives in Education*, Buckingham: Open University Press

Asmal, K. (2000) 'Message from the Minister of Education', in *The HIV/AIDS Emergency, Guidelines for Educators*, Pretoria: Department of Education

BBC News website (2004) *Teacher was Unfairly Dismissed* http://news. bbc.co.uk/go/pr/fr/-/1/hi/england/tyne/3496146.stm, 28 February

Barnard, N. (2000) 'Tory call for abuse charge anonymity', *Times Educational Supplement*, 16 June, p. 9

Bentham, M. (2000) 'Blair is wrong over Section 28 says Woodhead', *Sunday Telegraph*, 30 January, p. 1

Campbell, E. (2003) *The Ethical Teacher*, Maidenhead: Open University Press

Chitosi, I. (2000) 'Malawi must protect schoolgirls from sexual abuse', *Misanet.com/The Nation*, 30 October

Christian Institute (2001) *Cut the Clause: Teachers Should Not Have to Promote Gay Rights* July, Christian Institute

Clark, E. (2003) 'Kent acts to keep Section 28 alive in its schools', *Times Educational Supplement*, 1 August, p. 2

Cooper, M. and Curtis, B. (2000) *Managing Allegations against Staff Education: Personnel and Child Protection Issues in Schools*, Personnel Management Series, Stafford: Network Educational Press

Coward, R. (2001) 'Hogwarts, the haven', *Guardian*, 20 November, p. 18

Curcio, J. L., Berlin, L. F. and First, P. F. (1996) *Sexuality and the Schools: Handling the Critical Issues*, California: Corwin Press

Davidson, F. (2003) 'Ex "made life hell" ', *Times Educational Supplement*, Scotland 8 August, p. 6

Davies, C. (2003) *Majority of Students Molested by Teachers in Botswana* World Education Forum, UNESCO

Dean, C. (2000) 'Street baby not ministers' fault', *Times Educational Supplement*, 3 March, p. 6

Douglas, M. (1986) *Risk Acceptability according to the Social Sciences*, New York: Russell Sage Foundation

Duncan, N. (1999) *Sexual Bullying: Gender Conflict and Pupil Culture in Secondary Schools*, London: Routledge

Epstein, D. and Johnson, R. (1998) *Schooling Sexualities*, Buckingham: Open University Press

Farrell, M. (2003a) 'Sex case rise sparks "don't work alone" call', *Times Educational Supplement*, 19 September

Farrell, M. (2003b) 'Never teach alone, says MP', *Times Educational Supplement*, 19 September

Freedman, M. (2001) 'Face it: there is a war on', *Observer Business Section*, 18 November, p. 9

Freely, M. (2002) 'Sex education', *Guardian G2*, 5 February 2002, p. 4

Fryer, A. (2000) 'Boy wants damages in Letourneau rape case', *Seattle Times*, 14 April

General Teaching Council of England (2001) *Professional Code for Teachers: Draft Statement of Values and Practice*, London: GTC, May

General Teacher Council (England) (2002) *Code of Professional Values and Practice for Teachers*, London: GTCE, 27 February

Giddens, A. (1991) *Modernity and Self-Identity: Self and Society in the Late Modern Age*, Cambridge: Polity Press

Giddens, A. (1993) *The Transformation of Intimacy: Sexuality, Love and Eroticism in Modern Societies*, Cambridge: Polity Press

Glover, D. and Law, S. (1996) *Managing Professional Development in Education*, London: Kogan Page.

Goffe, L. (2003) 'Abused gays find refuge in school of their own', *Times Educational Supplement*, 8 August, p. 10

Greenfield, N. (2001) 'Schools let the abusers hunt on', *Times Educational Supplement*, 21 April, p. 5

Halstead, J. M. and Reiss, M. J. (2003) *Values in Sex Education: From Principles to Practice*, London: RoutledgeFalmer

Haydon, G. (1997) *Teaching about Values: A New Approach*, London: Cassell

Haynes, F. (1998) *The Ethical School*, London: Routledge

Hendrie, C. (2002) 'Aftermath of a murder trial', *Times Educational Supplement*, 18 January, p. 5

Hickson, A. (1995) *The Poisoned Bowl: Sex, Repression and the Public School System*, London: Constable

Hook, S. (1999) 'Forbidden Fruit', *Times Educational Supplement*. First Appointments, October 29, p. 13

Human Rights Watch, (2001) *Scared at School: Sexual Violence against Girls in South African Schools*, USA: Human Rights Watch: New York, Washington, London, Brussels. Copyright © March 2001 by Human Rights Watch. Library of Congress Control Number: 2001087292

Johnson, H. and Castelli, M. (1999) 'The National Professional Qualification for Head Teachers: the need for additional support for candidates for Catholic leadership', *Journal of In-service Education*, 25 (3): 519–532

Jones, A. (ed.) (2001) *Touchy Subject: Teachers Touching Children*, Dunedin, New Zealand: University of Otago Press

Jones, C. (1985) 'Sexual tyranny: male violence in a mixed secondary school', in Weiner, G. (ed.) *Just a Bunch of Girls*, Buckingham: Open University Press

Khayyat, M. D. (1992) *Lesbian Teachers: An Invisible Presence*, Albany, NY: State University of New York Press

Lees, S. (1987) 'The structure of sexual relations in school', in M. Arnot and G. Weiner, (eds) *Gender and the Politics of Schooling*, Buckingham: Open University Press

Lepkowska, D., Smith, N. and Stewart, W. (2003) 'Colleagues stress us out, say staff', *Times Educational Supplement*, 5 December, p. 3

Lerner, M. D., Volpe, J. S. and Lindell, B. (2003) *A Practical Guide for Crisis Response in Our Schools*, fifth edition, New York: American Academy of Experts in Traumatic Stress

Lott, P. (1996) 'Keeping up appearances', *Report Magazine*, Association of Teachers and Lecturers (ATL)

Lucas, S. (2004) 'Parents' fury at sex claim', *The Times Educational Supplement*, 12 March

MacBeath, J. (1988) *Personal and Social Education*, Edinburgh: Scottish Academic Press

MacBeath, J. (1999) *Schools Must Speak for Themselves*, London: Routledge

MacBeath, J. and Myers, K. (1999) *Effective School Leaders: How to Evaluate and Improve Your Leadership Potential*, London: Financial Times; Prentice Hall

McGettrick, B. J. (1994) 'Management and Values', in W. M. Humes and M. L. MacKenzie (eds) *The Management of Educational Policy: Scottish Perspectives*, Harlow: Longman

MacGilchrist, B., Myers, K. and Reed, J. (1997) *The Intelligent School*, London: Paul Chapman

McSmith, A. and Reeves, R. (2000) 'Gay law row that ignited Middle England', *Observer*, 30 January, pp. 10–11

McVeigh, T. (1999) 'Revealed: sex case teacher's obsessive past' and 'Cleared teacher was sexaholic', *Observer*, 14 November, pp. 1–2

Mahony, P. (1985) *Schools for the Boys? Co-education Reassessed*, London: Hutchinson

Murray, J. (2004) 'Fatal reaction', *Times Educational Supplement*, Jobs, 13 February

Neil, A. S. (1939) *The Problem Teacher*, London: Herbert Jenkins

O'Brien, J. and MacBeath, J. (1999) 'Coordinating staff development: the training and development of staff development coordinators', *Journal of In-service Education*, 25(1) 69–83

O'Brien, J. and Draper, J. (2003) 'Frameworks for CPD: the Chartered Teacher initiative in Scotland', *Professional Development Today*, 6, winter: 69–75.

Odone, C. (2002) 'Boys and girls come out to prey', *Observer*, 10 February p. 29

Ontario Ministry of Education (2001) *Ontario Schools: Code of Conduct*, Ottawa; Queen's Printer for Ontario, p. 5

Oram, A. (1996) *Women Teachers and Feminist Politics 1900–39*, Manchester: Manchester University Press

Oxford Encyclopedic English Dictionary (1991) Oxford: Oxford University Press

Petty, M. (2004) 'She undressed: I was out of my depth', *The Times*, T2 4 March p. 6

Piddocke, S., Magsino, R. and Manley-Casimir, M. (1997) *Teachers in Trouble: An Exploration of the Normative Character of Teaching*, Toronto: University of Toronto Press

Pilkington, M. (2004) 'Sexuality and the law', *Report Magazine*, Association of Teachers and Lecturers (ATL), p. 20

Rayner, S. (1992) *Cultural Theory and Risk Analysis*, in S. Krimsky and D. Golding (eds) *Social Theories of Risk*, Westport: Praeger, pp. 83–116

Revell, P. (2002) 'Safe sex: leave the kids alone', *Times Education Supplement*, Jobs, 1, Section 8, February

Rivers, R. (2000) Shattered Hopes: The Sexual Abuse of Girls in Botswana UNICEF

Scott, S. J. (2001), *Swings and Roundabouts: Risk Anxiety and the Everyday World of Children*, in A. Jones, (ed.) *Touchy Subject: Teachers Touching Children*, Dunedin, New Zealand: University of Otago Press, pp. 15–26

Scottish Executive Education Department (SEED) (2002) *The Standard for Chartered Teacher in Scotland*, Edinburgh: SEED

Scottish Office Education and Industry Department (SOEID) (1998) *The Standard for Headship in Scotland*, Stirling: SQH Unit.

Shoop, R. J. and Edwards, D. L (1994) *How to Stop Sexual Harassment in Our Schools: A Handbook and Curriculum Guide for Administrators and Teachers*, Needham Heights, Mass.: Allyn and Bacon

Skidelsky, R. (1969) *English Progressive Schools*, Penguin: Harmondsworth

Smith, P. (1997) 'Values and ethical issues in the management of continuing professional development', in H. Tomlinson (ed.) *Managing Continuing Professional Development in Schools*, London: Paul Chapman

South African Council of Educators (1999) *Code of Conduct for Educators*, Deutsche Schule, Pretoria: South African Council of Educators

Splevins, K. (2002) 'Girls at risk from sex abuse by teachers', *Times Educational Supplement*, 29 November, p. 16

Squirrell, G. (1989) 'Teachers and issues of sexual orientation', *Gender and Education*, 1(1): 17–34

Stephenson, J., Ling, L., Burman, E. and Cooper, M. (eds) (1998) *Values in Education*, London: Routledge

Stopes, M. (1926) *Sex and the Young*, London: Gill Publishing

Stronach, I., Corbin, B., McNamara, O., Stark S. and Warne T. (2002), 'Towards an uncertain politics of professionalism: teacher and nurse identities in flux', *Journal of Education Policy*, 17(1): 109–138

Teacher Training Agency (2003) *The New Induction Standards*, London: TTA

Times Educational Supplement Scotland (2003) 'Cupid's arrow', 8 August, p. 12

Tropp, A. (1957) *The School Teachers: The Growth of the Teaching Profession in England and Wales from 1800 to the Present Day*, London: William Heinemann

Wallace, J. (1997) 'Technologies of "the child": towards a theory of the child-subject', *Textual Practice*, 9(2): 285–302

Wallace, W. (2000) 'Four GCSEs and a baby', *Times Educational Supplement*, Friday 14 January, pp. 12–13

Wallace, W. (2000) 'I hated school: You have to put on an act every day', *Times Educational Supplement*, Friday, 3 March, pp. 8–10

Watson, B. and Ashton, E. (1995) *Education, Assumptions and Values*, London: David Fulton

Weaver, M. (1999) 'Teacher admits she did strip in front of boys', *Daily Telegraph*, 10 November, p. 5

Weaver, M. (1999) 'Woman teacher cleared of seducing pupil, 15', *Daily Telegraph*, 11 November, p. 1

Widdowson, F. (1980) *Going up into the Next Class: Women and elementary teacher training 1840–1914*, London: Hutchinson

Williams, C. (2000) 'Tricks of the trade: "How I dealt with a sex pest"', *Guardian*, March 8, p. 7

Williams, E. (2004) 'False accusations', *Times Educational Supplement*, Friday 20 February, pp. 11–14

Wolpe, A. M. (1988) *Within School Walls: The Role of Discipline, Sexuality and the Curriculum*, London: Routledge

Woods, K. (2000) *Sexual Abuse of Schoolgirls Widespread in Botswana*, Botswana Gazette/afrol.com, 15 November

Index